書下ろし

すらすら読める!

英語対訳・幕末維新史

木村幸比古 監修

Marilyn Lo 英文監訳

祥伝社黄金文庫

本書は、祥伝社黄金文庫のために書下ろされました。

装幀　鈴木大輔（ソウルデザイン）
本文まんが　山口ヒロフミ（MSデザイン）
編集協力　マイプラン

はじめに

本書は日本の歴史、とりわけ魅力的で、ファンも多い幕末維新史を英語で読む本です。英文は、初歩的な単語と文法で書かれており、下線の補助訳を参考にすれば、すらすら読めるでしょう。

章の終わりにあるクイズや巻末の英単語・英熟語集も英語学習には最適です。まんがなどもあり、楽しみながら1冊読み終える頃には、単語力を含め英語力がついている。そんな本です。

私の勤務する霊山歴史館は、幕末維新史を研究するはじめての専門博物館として、1970年に京都市に開館しました。西郷隆盛、高杉晋作など討幕派志士の遺品から新選組、徳川慶喜など幕府側の資料も数多くそろえています。

近年、外国人の方が多く来館され、外国語（そのほとんどが英語）で質問を受けます。彼らでなくとも、尊王攘夷、五箇条の誓文、大政奉還など歴史用語は英語にすると？　坂本龍馬や板垣退助の有名なセリフを英訳すると？　など興味はつきません。

「英語学習は、英文の内容に興味を持てなければ、頭に入りづらく効果的ではない」とは英語教育法の専門家であり、本書の英文監訳をお願いしたMarilyn Lo氏の言葉です。

本書で英語力を磨くとともに、近代日本を形づくった幕末維新を学び直されることを願ってやみません。母国語以外で母国の歴史を語る！　すばらしいではありませんか。

グローバル時代の新たな日本の夜明けに――。

霊山歴史館 学芸課長　木村幸比古

『すらすら読める！英語対訳・幕末維新史』目次

1章　黒船来航

2章　尊王攘夷運動

3章　戊辰戦争

4章　明治維新

5章　富国強兵

6章　文明開化

7章　自由民権運動

1章
黒船来航
The Arrival of Black Ships

1 The Arrival of Black Ships
黒船来航

① In June of 1853, four warships led by Perry, an
6月 軍艦 ～に率いられた
American Naval Chief in the East Indian Seas,
appeared off the coast of *Uraga* (*Yokosuka* City,
姿を現わした ～の沖に
Kanagawa Prefecture), which was at the mouth of *Edo*
入口
Bay. ② The Japanese were shocked at these huge Black
～に驚いた 巨大な
Ships. ③ Perry handed an official letter which was
渡した 正式な文書
written by the president of the United States to the
アメリカ大統領
officials of the shogunate, requesting the opening of
役人 幕府 要求した 開国
the country and trading with America. ④ Once the
通商
shogunate replied that it would give an answer the
返事をした
following year, Perry went away for a short period.
翌年 退去した 短いあいだ
⑤ In January of 1854, Perry visited again with seven

warships and strongly urged Japan to open its country.
強くせまった

⑥ The shogunate was compelled to agree to the
強制された　同意する

opening of Japan.

和訳

①1853年６月、江戸湾入口の浦賀(うらが)（神奈川県横須賀(よこすか)市）沖に、アメリカ海軍東インド艦隊司令長官・ペリーが率(ひき)いる４隻(せき)の軍艦が姿を現わしました。②日本人は、巨大な黒い軍艦に驚きました。③ペリーは、日本の開国と通商を求めるアメリカ大統領の国書を、江戸幕府側の役人に渡しました。④幕府は翌年に回答すると返答し、ペリーはいったん退去しました。⑤ペリーは、翌1854年１月、軍艦７隻を率いて再(ふたた)び来航し、開国を強くせまりました。⑥幕府は、開国要求を受け入れました。

2 The Opium War
アヘン戦争

① In 1840, the Opium War (アヘン戦争) occurred (起こった) between the Chinese *Qing* Dynasty (清朝) and the British Empire (イギリス). ② The British demanded (要求した) free trade (自由貿易) with China and started a war because China forced (強行した) the end of the Opium Trade (アヘン貿易) with the British. ③ China was defeated (敗れた) and the Treaty of *Nanking* (南京条約) was signed (調印した) in 1842. ④ The following year, China was forced to make unequal treaties (不平等条約) such as the agreement of extraterritoriality (領事裁判権) of the British in China and giving up the rights of tariff autonomy (関税自主権). ⑤ Afterward (その後), China was half colonized (半植民地化された) by being forced to sign the same treaties with the United States and the French Empire. ⑥ The result of this war had an impact on Japan, which was under the National Isolation Policy. ⑦ The *Edo* shogunate changed its policy to avoid wars with western countries by easing the decree for the repelling of foreign ships.

鎖国 / 江戸幕府 / 避ける / 緩和する / 異国船打払令

和訳

①1840年、中国清朝(しんちょう)とイギリスとのあいだでアヘン戦争が起こりました。②中国がイギリスとのアヘン貿易停止を強行したため、イギリスが中国との自由貿易を求めて開戦したのです。③中国は敗れ、1842年に南京(なんきん)条約を結びました。④翌年、中国はイギリスに領事(りょうじ)裁判権(さいばんけん)を認め、関税自主権(かんぜいじしゅけん)を放棄するという不平等条約を結ばされました。⑤その後、中国は同じ内容の条約を、アメリカ、フランスとも結ばされ、半植民地化が進みました。⑥アヘン戦争の結果は、鎖国(さこく)をしていた日本に衝撃を与えました。⑦江戸幕府は、異国船打払令(いこくせんうちはらいれい)を緩和(かんわ)し、欧米との武力衝突を避ける政策へと転換しました。

3 The Japan-US Treaty of Peace and Amity and the Opening of the Country

日米和親条約と開国

（にちべいわしん）

① Japan made the Treaty of Peace and Amity with the
和親条約
United States in March of 1854. ② Under this treaty,
条約
Japan opened two ports: *Shimoda* (Now *Shimoda* City,
Shizuoka Prefecture) and *Hakodate* (Now *Hakodate*
静岡県
City, *Hokkaido*), and agreed to the residence of the U.S.
～に同意した 駐在
consul. ③ Japan also promised to supply fuel and food
領事 約束した 供給する
to American ships and recognized America as the most
認めた 最恵国
favored nation. ④ This most favored nation treatment
待遇
means that if Japan makes a treaty with other countries
with more favorable conditions than America, America
有利な 条件
can automatically be applied the same conditions.
自動的に 適用される
⑤ Afterward, Japan concluded similar treaties with
締結した 類似した

England, Russia and the Netherlands. ⑥ As a result, Japan decided to stop the National Isolation Policy, which had lasted for about 200 years, and open Japan to foreign countries.

the Netherlands: オランダ
As a result: その結果
decided: 決定した
the National Isolation Policy: 鎖国政策

和訳

①1854年３月、日本はアメリカとのあいだに日米和親条約を結びました。②この条約で、日本は下田（しもだ）（現・静岡県下田市）と箱館（はこだて）（現・北海道函館市）の２港を開港し、領事の駐在を認めました。③また、アメリカ船に燃料や食料を供給することを約束し、アメリカに対して最恵国待遇（さいけいこくたいぐう）を認めました。④最恵国待遇とは、日本がほかの国とアメリカよりも有利な条件で条約を結んだ場合は、アメリカにも自動的にその条件を認めるというものでした。⑤その後、日本は同じ内容の条約をイギリス、ロシア、オランダとも結びました。⑥その結果、約200年間続いた鎖国政策をやめ、開国することになりました。

4 Unequal Treaties
不平等条約

① A U.S. Consul General, Harris, who stayed in Japan
アメリカ総領事
under the Japan-US Treaty of Peace and Amity, strongly
日米和親条約
demanded that Japan sign the Treaty of Commerce.
要求した 通商条約
② In 1858, the chief minister of the *Edo* shogunate,
大老
Ii Naosuke, signed the Japan-US Treaty of Amity and
日米修好通商条約
Commerce on his own judgment without permission
独断 許可
of the Imperial Court. ③ Japan opened the ports of
朝廷
Kanagawa, *Nagasaki*, *Niigata*, *Hakodate* and *Hyogo*
under this treaty. ④ Moreover, this was an unequal
そのうえ 不平等条約
treaty with the agreement of extraterritoriality and no
領事裁判権
rights of tariff autonomy. ⑤ As a result, the crimes
関税自主権 犯罪
committed by Americans in Japan were judged by the
犯された

American Consul. ⑥ Tariff was discussed and decided
アメリカ領事　関税　協議した

by both countries. ⑦ The shogunate made similar
幕府

treaties with the Netherlands, Russia, England and France, and Japan started to trade with western countries.

和訳

①日米和親条約によって日本に駐在したアメリカ総領事・ハリスは、日本に対して通商条約を結ぶことを強く要求しました。②1858年、大老(たいろう)・井伊直弼(いいなおすけ)は朝廷の許可なく、独断で日米修好通商(しゅうこうつうしょう)条約を結びました。③この条約で、日本は神奈川、長崎、新潟、箱館、兵庫を開港しました。④またこの条約は、領事裁判権を認め、関税自主権のない不平等条約でした。⑤この結果、日本国内におけるアメリカ人の犯罪は、アメリカ領事が裁判することになりました。⑥関税は両国の協議によって決められました。⑦幕府は、オランダ、ロシア、イギリス、フランスとも同じ内容の条約を結び、日本は欧米諸国との貿易を開始しました。

5

Yoshida Shoin and Shokason Juku

吉田松陰（よしだしょういん）と松下村塾（しょうかそんじゅく）

① *Yoshida Shoin*, who was a samurai in lower ranks (下級) in the *Choshu* Domain (長州藩), learned Holland studies from *Sakuma Shozan*, a scholar (学者) of Western studies. ② Although (けれども) he secretly planned to go abroad (海外へ行く) in 1854 when Perry arrived again, he failed (失敗した) and was locked up (幽閉された) in *Hagi*. ③ Later, he inherited (受け継いだ) *Shokason Juku* from his uncle who started to open the *juku*, and had a discussion with his many followers (弟子). ④ *Shokason Juku* was a private cram school (私塾), and anyone could be equally (平等に) educated (教育を受けた) with no rank difference there. ⑤ Many people who actively worked at the end of the shogunate (幕末) and in the Restoration Period (維新) such as *Takasugi Shinsaku*,

Kusaka Genzui, *Ito Hirobumi* and *Yamagata Aritomo* graduated from the *juku*. ⑥ *Yoshida Shoin* was one of the Radical supporters of Nationalistic Imperialism. ⑦ He was executed during the *Ansei* Period Purge done by *Ii Naosuke*.

卒業した

急進的な尊王攘夷派

処刑された

安政の大獄

和訳

①もと長州藩下級武士だった吉田松陰は、洋学者の佐久間象山から蘭学を学びました。②1854年、ペリー再航の際に密航を企てましたが失敗し、萩で幽閉されました。③その後、吉田松陰は叔父が開いた松下村塾を受け継ぎ、多くの弟子と意見を交わしました。④松下村塾は、身分の別なく、誰でも平等に教育を受けられる私塾でした。⑤松下村塾は、高杉晋作、久坂玄瑞、伊藤博文、山県有朋ら、幕末維新期に活躍した多くの人物を輩出しました。⑥吉田松陰は急進的な尊王攘夷派でした。⑦井伊直弼による安政の大獄で処刑されてしまいました。

6 Succession Problems of the Shogun

将軍継嗣（けいし）問題

① The 13th shogun, *Tokugawa Iesada* was physically
13代将軍 身体的に
weak and had no children to become his successor.
あとつぎ
② Two people were recommended as the next shogun.
推薦された
③ They were *Hitotsubashi Yoshinobu* from the *Mito*
水戸藩
Domain and *Tokugawa Yoshitomi* from the *Kishu*
Domain. ④ Those that recommended *Hitotsubashi*
Yoshinobu were *Matsudaira Yoshinaga*, the lord of
福井藩主
Fukui Domain, and *Abe Masahiro*, a senior councillor
老中
of the shogunate who mainly led the *Hitotsubashi*
率いた 一橋派
group. ⑤ The lord of *Hikone* Domain, *Ii Naosuke* who
mainly led the *Nanki* group recommended *Tokugawa*
Yoshitomi. ⑥ The situation had completely changed
完全に

once *Ii Naosuke* from the *Nanki* group took the position of the chief minister of the *Edo* shogunate.
大老
⑦ *Ii Naosuke* decided that *Tokugawa Yoshitomi* was the next successor. ⑧ *Yoshitomi* became *Tokugawa Iemochi*, the 14th shogun.

和訳

①13代将軍・徳川家定は病弱なうえ、あとつぎとなる子がいませんでした。②次期将軍の候補には、２人の人物が推されました。③水戸藩の一橋慶喜と、紀州藩の徳川慶福です。④一橋慶喜を推したのは、福井藩主の松平慶永や、老中の阿部正弘を中心とした一橋派でした。⑤徳川慶福を推したのは、彦根藩主の井伊直弼を中心とした南紀派でした。⑥南紀派の井伊直弼が大老に就くと状況は一変しました。⑦井伊直弼は、徳川慶福をあとつぎと定めました。⑧慶福は、14代将軍・徳川家茂となりました。

7 The Ansei Period Purge

安政(あんせい)の大獄(たいごく)

① *Ii Naosuke*, the chief minister of the *Edo* shogunate,
大老
signed the Japan-US Treaty of Amity and Commerce
日米修好通商条約
without the permission of the Imperial Court in 1858.
朝廷
② As for the succession problem of the shogun, he
将軍継嗣問題
gave *Tokugawa Iemochi* the position as successor by
making use of the power of the *Tairo*. ③ There were
～を利用して
criticisms toward assertive *Ii Naosuke*. ④ *Ii Naosuke*
非難 独断的な
strictly cracked down on feudal lords, feudal warriors
厳しく ～を取り締まった 大名 藩士
and court nobles of the *Hitotsubashi* group that
公家
opposed him, and punished them. ⑤ This is called "The
対立した 処罰した
Ansei Period Purge". ⑥ Meanwhile, *Yoshida Shoin* of
安政の大獄 そのあいだ
the *Choshu* Domain who supported Nationalistic
尊王攘夷

Imperialism, was executed (処刑された). ⑦ The feudal warriors of the *Choshu* Domain (長州藩士) who followed *Yoshida Shoin* felt resentment (恨み) against this and started to activate the Nationalistic Imperialism movement.

和訳

①1858年、大老・井伊直弼は、朝廷の許可を得ないまま日米修好通商条約を締結（ていけつ）しました。②将軍継嗣問題では、大老の強権を発動して徳川家茂をあとつぎに決めました。③強引な井伊直弼に対し、非難の声が上がりました。④井伊直弼は、将軍継嗣問題で対立していた一橋派の大名・藩士・公家（くげ）を厳しく取り締まり、処罰しました。⑤これを「安政の大獄」といいます。⑥この時、尊王攘夷論を主張していた長州藩の吉田松陰が処刑されました。⑦吉田松陰に師事していた長州藩士たちは恨（うら）みを持ち、尊王攘夷運動を活発化させました。

8 The Sakurada Gate Incident

桜田門外の変（さくらだもんがい）

Prepare to die!
覚悟せよ！
1860年、江戸城桜田門外で、水戸浪士らが井伊直弼を襲い、暗殺しました。

The power of the shogunate has become weak.
幕府の力も弱くなったものだ。
ガラガラ
桜田門外の変は、幕府の権威の失墜をもたらしました。

The Imperial Court and the shogunate should cooperate with each other!
朝廷と幕府は協力すべきだ！
幕府は、薩摩藩の島津久光を中心に公武合体を進め、幕政の改革を行ないました。

おさらいクイズ

【問題1】次の英語が表わす日本語を、あとのア〜ウから選びなさい。

① shogunate
② domain
③ feudal lord

ア 大名　イ 幕府　ウ 藩

【問題2】次の日本語が表わす英語を、あとのア〜ウから選びなさい。

① 鎖国
② 関税自主権
③ 領事裁判権

ア extraterritoriality
イ tariff autonomy
ウ the National Isolation Policy

【問題3】次の英文の意味を、あとのア〜ウから選びなさい。

The crimes committed by Americans in Japan were judged by the American Consul.

ア 日本国内におけるアメリカ人の犯罪は、アメリカ領事によって裁判されました。
イ 日本国内におけるアメリカ人の犯罪は、日本の法律によって裁判されました。
ウ アメリカ人に対する日本人の犯罪は、アメリカ領事によって裁判されました。

【問題4】次の日本語を英文にしたものを、あとのア〜ウから選びなさい。

吉田松陰は井伊直弼によって処刑されました。

ア *Yoshida Shoin* learned Holland studies from *Ii Naosuke*.
イ *Yoshida Shoin* had a discussion with *Ii Naosuke*.
ウ *Yoshida Shoin* was executed by *Ii Naosuke*.

【問題5】次の英文の(　)にあてはまる1語を書きなさい。

Tokugawa Yoshitomi (　　) *Tokugawa Iemochi*, the 14th shogun.
徳川慶福は、14代将軍・徳川家茂となりました。

2章
尊王攘夷運動
The Nationalistic Imperialism Movement

【答え1】①イ　②ウ　③ア　【答え2】①ウ　②イ　③ア　【答え3】ア
【答え4】ウ　【答え5】became

9 Union of the Imperial Court and the Shogunate, and the Marriage of the Emperor's Sister, Kazunomiya with the Shogun

こう ぶ がったい かずのみやこうか
公武合体政策と和宮降嫁

① The leadership of the shogunate remarkably
著しく
weakened after *Ii Naosuke* was assassinated outside
暗殺された
the *Sakurada* Gate. ② *Ando Nobumasa*, a senior
老中
councillor of the shogunate, and the others made a
plan to greet Emperor *Komei's* sister, Princess
孝明天皇の 和宮親子内親王
Kazunomiya Chikako as the first lady of the 14th
shogun, *Tokugawa Iemochi*. ③ They intended to restore
～しようと思った 回復する
the dignity of the shogunate by utilizing the authority
威厳 利用 権威
of the Imperial Court. ④ *Kazunomiya* had a fiancé
named Prince *Arisugawanomiya Taruhito*. ⑤ At first,
有栖川宮熾仁親王
Emperor *Komei* declined the request of the marriage
断わった
with *Kazunomiya*. ⑥ The court noble, *Iwakura Tomomi*

and the others supported the marriage of *Kazunomiya* because they considered (考えた) it as an opportunity (機会) of strengthening their right of having a say (発言権) in the shogunate toward the Imperial Court. ⑦ The Imperial Court accepted (受諾した) the marriage in exchange with the conditions of the realization (実現) of expelling foreigners (攘夷) and the breach (破棄) of treaty.

和訳

①桜田門外の変で井伊直弼を失い、幕府の求心力は著(いちじる)しく低下していました。②老中・安藤信正(あんどうのぶまさ)らは、14代将軍・徳川家茂の正室に、孝明天皇の妹である和宮親子内親王(ちかこないしんのう)を迎える計画を立てました。③朝廷の権威を利用し、幕府の威信を回復しようと考えたのです。④和宮には、有栖川宮熾仁親王(ありすがわのみやたるひと)という婚約者がいました。⑤孝明天皇は、一度は和宮の降嫁を断わりました。⑥公家の岩倉具視(いわくらともみ)らは、これを機に朝廷の幕府に対する発言権を高めようと考え、和宮の降嫁を後押ししました。⑦朝廷は、攘夷の実行と条約破棄という条件を幕府に突きつけ、和宮の降嫁を承諾しました。

10 The Nationalistic Imperialism Movement

尊王攘夷運動

① The shogunate was forced to open its country by yielding to the pressure of foreign countries. ② Within the country, a nationalistic opinion that foreigners should be expelled was raised. ③ Furthermore, nationalism was connected with imperialism (revering the Emperor), and the idea of "Nationalistic Imperialism" was formed. ④ It was the *Mito*, the *Satsuma* and the *Choshu* Domains that actively pushed the Nationalistic Imperialism Movement. ⑤ The shogunate promoted the policy of uniting the court and the shogunate under the leadership of *Ando Nobumasa*, a senior councillor of the shogunate.

was forced to：強要された
yielding to：～に屈した
Within the country：国内では
a nationalistic opinion that foreigners should be expelled：攘夷論
was raised：持ち上がった
Furthermore：さらに
imperialism (revering the Emperor)：尊王論
Nationalistic Imperialism：尊王攘夷
the Nationalistic Imperialism Movement：尊王攘夷運動
promoted：進めた（促進した）
the policy of uniting the court and the shogunate：公武合体政策

⑥ However, the radical group of Nationalistic
急進的尊王攘夷派

Imperialism reacted against this policy, and *Ando*
～に反発した

Nobumasa was attacked by the members of the *Mito*
～によって攻撃された　水戸藩士

Domain and got injured in 1862. ⑦ This is called "the
負傷した

Incident Outside the *Sakashita* Gate".
坂下門外の変

和訳

①幕府は、諸外国の圧力に屈する形で開国を余儀(よぎ)なくされました。②国内では、夷人(いじん)(外国人)を打ち払おうという攘夷論が持ち上がりました。③さらに攘夷論は天皇を尊(とうと)ぶ尊王論と結びつき、「尊王攘夷」という考えかたが生まれました。④尊王攘夷運動を推進したのは水戸、薩摩、長州の各藩でした。⑤幕府は、老中・安藤信正のもと、公武合体の政策を進めました。⑥しかし、この政策に急進的な尊王攘夷派は反発し、安藤信正は1862年、水戸藩士の襲撃を受け、負傷しました。⑦これが「坂下(さかした)門外の変」です。

11 The Teradaya Incident
寺田屋事件

① In 1862, the *Satsuma* feudal lord and the father of
薩摩藩主
Shimazu Tadayoshi, *Hisamitsu* headed for *Kyoto* with
～へ向かった
1,000 warriors in order to reform the shogunate
～するために 改革する
government. ② The members of expelling foreigners
攘夷
expected *Shimazu Hisamitsu* to realize the anti-
期待した 実現する 反幕・攘夷
shogunate nationalism. ③ However, *Shimazu*
Hisamitsu's aim was the Union of the Imperial Court
ねらい 公武合体政策
and the shogunate. ④ *Arima Shinshichi* and others
from the extremists in the *Satsuma* Domain got together
過激派
at *Teradaya* Inn for sailors in *Fushimi* with a plot to
寺田屋 暗殺計画
assassinate *Kujo Hisatada*, a court noble from the
policy group of uniting the court and the shogunate,
公武合体派

and *Sakai Tadaaki*, the local governor of *Kyoto*.
京都所司代

⑤ *Shimazu Hisamitsu* sent the domain members to *Teradaya* to stop the disturbance. ⑥ *Arima Shinshichi* and others refused the persuasion, which led to a battle of killing each other. ⑦ *Arima Shinshichi* was killed and the action of the extremists was prevented.

騒ぎ　断わった　説得　～を引きおこした　斬り合い　過激派　防がれた

和訳

①1862年、薩摩藩主・島津忠義（ただよし）の父である久光は、幕政改革を行なうため、1000人の兵を率いて京都へ向かいました。②攘夷派の志士は、島津久光に反幕・攘夷の実行を期待していました。③しかし、島津久光のねらいは公武合体政策でした。④有馬新七（ありましんしち）ら薩摩藩の過激派は、公武合体派の公家・九条尚忠（くじょうひさただ）や、京都所司代（しょしだい）の酒井忠義（さかいただあき）の暗殺を計画し、伏見（ふしみ）の船宿・寺田屋に集結していました。⑤島津久光は、計画を押さえようと寺田屋に藩士を送りました。⑥有馬新七らは説得を拒否し、薩摩藩士どうしの斬（き）り合いとなりました。⑦有馬新七らは討（う）たれ、過激派の行動は防がれました。

12 The Birth of Shinsen-gumi

新選組の誕生

① In 1862, the shogun, *Iemochi* was planning to visit
Kyoto. ② The shogunate formed a lordless samurai
結成した　浪士組
group as guards. ③ The formation was suggested by
〜によって提案された
Kiyokawa Hachiro of the *Shonai* Domain. ④ The
reason for the formation of the *Roshi-gumi* by
Kiyokawa Hachiro was to make use of them in the
〜を利用する
movement of expelling foreigners. ⑤ The shogunate
攘夷運動
called them back to *Edo*. ⑥ *Kondo Isami* and *Hijikata*
Toshizo stayed in *Kyoto* in order to guard the shogun
〜するために　守る
with all their might. ⑦ They formed "the *Shinsen-*
全力で
gumi". ⑧ The *Shinsen-gumi* took the position of
〜に就任した
maintaining the security of *Kyoto* under the supervision
治安維持　管理

of the office of *Kyoto* protectors in the *Aizu* Domain.
京都守護職

⑨ The *Shinsen-gumi* showed achievements at the
功績をあげた

time of the *Ikedaya* Incident in 1864 and the *Kinmon*
池田屋事件 禁門の変

Incident.

和訳

①1862年、将軍・家茂が上洛(じょうらく)することになりました。②幕府は将軍を警護するために浪士組(ろうしぐみ)を結成しました。③浪士組の結成は、庄内(しょうない)藩の清河八郎(きよかわはちろう)の提案によるものでした。④清河八郎が浪士組を結成したのは、攘夷運動に利用するためでした。⑤幕府は浪士組を江戸に呼び戻しました。⑥浪士組のうち、近藤勇(こんどういさみ)、土方歳三(ひじかたとしぞう)らは、将軍の警護を全(まっと)うするとして京都に残りました。⑦彼らは「新選組」を結成しました。⑧新選組は、京都守護職をつとめる会津(あいづ)藩の管理のもと、京都の治安維持の任務につきました。⑨新選組は、1864年の池田屋事件や禁門(きんもん)の変などで功績をあげました。

13 The Namamugi Incident and the Anglo-Satsuma War

生麦(なまむぎ)事件と薩英(さつえい)戦争

① It was a time in 1862, when *Shimazu Hisamitsu*, a
man with power of the *Satsuma* Domain, was moving
実力者
from *Edo* to *Kyoto*. ② An Englishman named
Richardson and his men on horses were getting in the
馬に乗った　さえぎろうとして
way of a procession of *Shimazu Hisamitsu's* party in the
行列
village of *Namamugi* (now *Namamugi*, *Tsurumi* Ward,
鶴見区
Yokohama City). ③ The members of the *Satsuma*
横浜市
Domain told them to get off from their horses and give
〜から降りる
the right of way. ④ However, they didn't understand
道をゆずる　しかし
Japanese, so Richardson and his men didn't get off.
⑤ The members of the *Satsuma* Domain struck them
斬った
with swords. ⑥ Richardson died and two were seriously
刀　重傷を負った

injured. ⑦ This is called "the *Namamugi* Incident". ⑧ In 1863, England attacked the *Satsuma* Domain by firing guns from the warships as an act of revenge (the Anglo-*Satsuma* War). ⑨ Upon witnessing the military strength of England, the *Satsuma* Domain changed its policy from expelling foreigners toward opening Japan.

生麦事件 砲撃 艦隊 手段 報復 薩英戦争 目撃 軍事力 攘夷 開国

和訳

①1862年、薩摩藩の実力者・島津久光が、江戸から京都へ移動している時でした。②生麦村(現・横浜市鶴見区生麦)で、島津久光の行列を、乗馬中のイギリス人のリチャードソンらがさえぎろうとしました。③薩摩藩士は、馬を降りて道をゆずるよう彼らに伝えました。④しかし言葉が通じず、リチャードソンらは馬から降りませんでした。⑤薩摩藩士は、彼らを斬りつけました。⑥リチャードソンは死亡し、２人が重傷を負いました。⑦これが「生麦事件」です。⑧1863年、イギリスは報復として艦隊による薩摩藩への砲撃を行ないました(薩英戦争)。⑨イギリスの軍事力を目(ま)の当(あ)たりにし、薩摩藩の方針は攘夷から開国に傾きました。

14 The Coup of August 18
八月十八日の政変

① The members of the Nationalistic Imperialism group (尊王攘夷派) from the *Choshu* Domain were making a radical (過激な) plan in *Kyoto*. ② They were trying to appeal directly (直訴する) to Emperor *Komei* (孝明天皇) for ordering the *Tokugawa* shogunate and the feudal lords (大名) to carry out (決行する) the action of expelling foreigners. ③ They intended to start the anti-shogunate movement (倒幕運動) under the name of (〜の名のもとに) the Imperial Court (朝廷) if the shogunate refused to do so. ④ The court nobles from the policy group of uniting the court and the shogunate (公武合体派), with the *Aizu* and the *Satsuma* Domains being the primary members, made a plan to expel (追放する) the radical court nobles (急進派の公家) and the *Choshu* Domain. ⑤ The warriors from the *Aizu* and *Satsuma* Domains closed the Imperial Palace (御所) and expelled the members of the *Choshu* Domain on August 18, 1863. ⑥ The seven radical court nobles, who supported *Choshu*, lost their positions (失脚した) and were expelled from Kyoto, and they ran away (逃げた) to the *Choshu* Domain with its members.

和訳

①尊王攘夷派の長州藩士たちは京都で過激な計画を立てていました。②孝明天皇に対し、徳川幕府と諸大名に攘夷決行を命ずるよう直訴（じきそ）しようとしていたのです。③幕府が拒否すれば、朝廷の名のもとに倒幕行動を起こすつもりでした。④公武合体派の公家や会津藩・薩摩藩を中心に、急進派の公家と長州藩の京都追放が計画されました。⑤1863年８月18日、会津・薩摩藩の兵が御所（ごしょ）を閉鎖し、長州藩士を締め出しました。⑥長州藩についていた急進派の７人の公家は失脚し、京都から追放され、長州藩士らとともに長州藩へと落ちのびました。

15 The Ikedaya Incident
池田屋事件

Our fellows seem to have been caught.
仲間が捕まったらしい。
池田屋では、長州藩の藩士や志士などが集まり、打ち合わせをしていました。
Oh no!
たいへんだ!
池田屋のまわりを会津藩兵が取り囲み、新選組は池田屋に乗り込みました。
Prepare to die!
覚悟！
長州藩らの藩士たちは、全員が死亡・捕縛(ほばく)されました。

16 The Kinmon Incident
禁門の変

① The *Choshu* Domain was expelled (追放された) from *Kyoto* in the Coup of August 18. (八月十八日の政変) ② Some from the radical group (急進派) such as *Kusaka Genzui* and *Kijima Matabei* came to *Kyoto* to attack and defeat (退ける) the *Aizu* and *Satsuma* Domains. ③ On the other side (いっぽう), *Takasugi Shinsaku*, *Katsura Kogoro* (*Kido Takayoshi*) and others, supported the Conservative Policy (慎重論). ④ However, once news broke out (発生した) and spread (広まった) that the members of the *Choshu* Domain were killed in the *Ikedaya* Incident (池田屋事件), they were unable to stop the radical group. ⑤ The members of the *Choshu* Domain dispatched troops (出兵した) and headed for (〜に向かって進んだ) *Kyoto*. ⑥ The troops of *Choshu* (長州勢) entered *Kyoto*, well prepared (準備した)

themselves, and started the war near the *Hamaguri* 蛤御門 Gate of the Imperial Palace. 御所 ⑦ The *Choshu* Domain was utterly defeated 惨敗した after they fought with the *Aizu* Domain, *Shinsen-gumi* and the *Satsuma* Domain.

和訳

①八月十八日の政変で、長州藩は京都から追放されました。②久坂玄瑞、来島又兵衛（きじままたべえ）ら急進派は、京都へ攻め上り、会津藩や薩摩藩を退（しりぞ）けようと考えました。③いっぽう、高杉晋作や桂小五郎（かつらこごろう）（木戸孝允（きどたかよし））らは、慎重論を唱えていました。④しかし、池田屋事件で長州藩士が犠牲となったことが伝わると、急進派をおさえることができなくなりました。⑤長州藩士は京都に向けて出兵しました。⑥長州勢は京都に入って準備を整え、御所の蛤御門（はまぐりごもん）付近で戦いを開始しました。⑦長州藩は、会津藩や新選組、薩摩藩を相手に戦いましたが、惨敗しました。

17 The First War between the Shogunate and the Choshu Domain (The First Choshu Expedition)

第一次幕長戦争（第一次長州征討）

① As the *Choshu* Domain came to attack the Imperial Palace (御所) against the order of (～の命令) the Imperial Court (朝廷) in the *Kinmon* Incident (禁門の変) in 1864, it was considered (みなされた) as the enemy of the Imperial Court (朝敵). ② The Imperial Court ordered the shogunate to track down and destroy (追討する) the *Choshu* Domain. ③ The shogunate (幕府) dispatched troops mainly from the *Satsuma* Domain. ④ The *Choshu* Domain had no extra power (余力) fighting against the shogunate because it was a time right after its defeat in the *Kinmon* Incident. ⑤ In the *Choshu* Domain, the conservative group (保守派) replaced the radical wing (急進派) to take leadership (主導権を握る). ⑥ The *Choshu* Domain made an apology (謝罪した)

to the shogunate. ⑦ The shogunate military withdrew its troops because the *Choshu* Domain showed obedience to the shogunate.

幕府軍 撤兵した 服従

和訳

①1864年の禁門の変で、長州藩は朝廷の命令に逆らって御所に攻め入ったため、朝敵（ちょうてき）とされました。②朝廷は、幕府に対し、長州藩を追討（ついとう）するよう命じました。③幕府は、薩摩藩を中心に出兵しました。④長州藩は、禁門の変で敗れた直後であり、幕府に対し対抗する余力がありませんでした。⑤長州藩内では、勢力を失った急進派に代わり、保守派が主導権を握っていました。⑥長州藩は、幕府に謝罪しました。⑦長州軍が幕府に従う姿勢を示したため、幕府軍は撤兵（てっぺい）しました。

18

The Bomb Battle by the Four Countries' Allied Fleet in Shimonoseki

四カ国連合艦隊下関(しものせき)砲撃事件

① The *Choshu* Domain carried out (実行した) the expelling of foreigners (攘夷) in 1863. ② They attacked all foreign ships passing the *Shimonoseki* Strait (下関海峡) by bombs indiscriminately (無差別に). ③ Four countries, which were England, France, America and the Netherlands, decided (決定した) to retaliate (報復する) against this. ④ The four countries formed (編成した) an allied fleet (連合艦隊) and started to attack gun batteries (砲台) of the *Choshu* Domain. ⑤ The allied fleet destroyed main gun batteries of the *Choshu* Domain only in one day. ⑥ All of the gun batteries were occupied (占拠された) and the *Choshu* Domain was utterly defeated (惨敗した). ⑦ This defeat, together with the loss (敗北) in the *Kinmon* Incident (禁門の変) caused severe (～に大きな打撃を与えた)

damage to the *Choshu* Domain. ⑧ The *Choshu* Domain gave up expelling foreigners and started a step toward modernization by deepening its relationship with foreign countries.

gave up：あきらめた　modernization：近代化　deepening：深めること　relationship：関係

和訳

①1863年、長州藩は攘夷を実行しました。②下関海峡を通過する外国船に対し、無差別砲撃を行なったのです。③これに対し、イギリス・フランス・アメリカ・オランダの四カ国は報復を行なうことを決定しました。④四カ国は連合艦隊を編成し、長州藩の砲台に対して砲撃を開始しました。⑤連合艦隊は、たった1日で長州藩の主要な砲台を破壊しました。⑥砲台はすべて占拠（せんきょ）され、長州藩は四カ国連合艦隊に惨敗しました。⑦禁門の変での敗北と合わせて、この敗戦は長州藩に大きな打撃を与えました。⑧長州藩は攘夷を捨て、外国との関係を深め、近代化への道を歩み始めることとなりました。

19 Irregular Military, Naval Forces, and Land Forces

奇兵隊、海援隊、陸援隊

① As the *Choshu* Domain knew the power difference
of military forces of other foreign countries, they
諸外国の軍隊
formed the irregular military led by *Takasugi*
奇兵隊 ～に率いられた
Shinsaku. ② The military accepted anyone regardless
受け入れた ～に関係なく
of the difference in social status, such as peasants and
身分 農民
townspeople, with the exception of feudal warriors.
町民 藩士
③ The irregular military was active in the Second War between the Shogunate and the *Choshu* Domain (The Second *Choshu* Expedition), and in the *Boshin* War.
戊辰戦争
④ Around the same time, in the *Tosa* Domain, the
naval forces where *Sakamoto Ryoma* was the
海援隊
commander, and the landing forces led by *Nakaoka*
隊長 陸援隊

Shintaro, were established. ⑤ The naval and landing
結成された

forces devoted to the anti-shogunate movement, as an
〜に尽くした 倒幕運動

affiliated organization. ⑥ The naval forces led the
外郭団体

fleet to fight with the shogunate military in the Second War between the Shogunate and the *Choshu* Domain and contributed greatly to the victory of the *Choshu* Domain.
貢献した

和訳

①諸外国との軍事力の差を知った長州藩は、高杉晋作を中心として奇兵隊を組織しました。②奇兵隊は、身分にとらわれずに、藩士以外の農民や町民も兵として加えました。③奇兵隊は、第二次幕長戦争(第二次長州征討)や戊辰(ぼしん)戦争などで活躍しました。④同じ頃、土佐藩では坂本龍馬を隊長とする海援隊、中岡慎太郎(なかおかしんたろう)を隊長とする陸援隊が結成されました。⑤海援隊や陸援隊は、土佐藩の外郭(がいかく)団体として、倒幕運動に尽力しました。⑥海援隊は、第二次幕長戦争の際、軍艦を率いて幕府軍と戦い、長州藩の勝利に大きく貢献しました。

20 The Eight Outlines Laid Down on a Ship

船中八策

① *Goto Shojiro* of the *Tosa* Domain thought that if
考えた
the shogunate was overthrown, the *Tosa* Domain,
転覆した
which was supportive of the shogunate, would become
〜に協力的な
insecure in the new administration. ② *Sakamoto*
不安定な 新政権
Ryoma proposed to *Goto Shojiro*, "The Idea of the
〜に提案した
Restoration of Imperial Rule". ③ *Goto Shojiro* and
大政奉還
Sakamoto Ryoma departed *Nagasaki* port in order to
港 〜のために
offer the Restoration of Imperial Rule to the former
提言する 前土佐藩主
lord of the *Tosa* Domain, *Yamauchi Toyoshige* (*Youdou*)

in *Kyoto*. ④ *Sakamoto Ryoma* planned the basic ideas
基本理念
of a new government on board a ship. ⑤ They were
新政権 船中で
the establishment of a parliament and a constitution,
議会 憲法

a recruitment of talented people, the amendment of
採用 有能な 不平等条約の改定

unequal treaties, the reinforcement of naval forces, the
増強 海軍

disposition of imperial guard troops, and the change
設置 御親兵

of the exchange rate between gold and silver. ⑥ This
交換レート

is called "the Eight Outlines Laid Down on a Ship".
船中八策

和訳

①土佐藩の後藤象二郎(ごとうしょうじろう)は、武力討幕が実現すると、幕府に対して好意的な土佐藩の新政権内での立場が危(あや)うくなると考えました。②坂本龍馬は、後藤象二郎に「大政奉還案」を提言しました。③後藤象二郎と坂本龍馬は、京都にいた前土佐藩主・山内豊信(やまうちとよしげ)(容堂(ようどう))に大政奉還を提言するため、長崎から出航しました。④船中で、坂本龍馬は新政権の基本理念を示しました。⑤議会の設置、憲法の制定、有能な人材の登用、不平等条約改正、海軍力の増強、御親兵(ごしんぺい)の設置、金銀交換レートの変更といった内容でした。⑥これを「船中八策」といいます。

21

The Satsuma-Choshu Alliance

薩長同盟

There is a need for a union of the *Satsuma* and the *Choshu* Domains!
薩摩藩と長州藩の同盟が必要なんだ！
坂本龍馬は西郷隆盛を説得し、なんとか会談にこぎつけました。
We have no time to think about the pride of our Domain!
藩のメンツにこだわっている場合じゃない！
同盟の話を切り出そうとしない双方を、坂本龍馬が一喝（いっかつ）しました。
Let's forgive and forget what happened in our past.
今までのことは水に流そう。
Our feeling is mutual. Thank you.
こちらこそ、よろしく。
薩摩藩から同盟を切り出す形で、薩長同盟は結ばれました。1866年1月、長州藩の名誉回復と討幕のために両者は手を結んだのです。

22 The Second War between the Shogunate and the Choshu Domain (The Second Choshu Expedition)

第二次幕長戦争（第二次長州征討）

① The shogunate couldn't finish the *Choshu* Domain
幕府
off in the First War between the Shogunate and the
第一次幕長戦争
Choshu Domain of 1864 because they surrendered at
降伏した
once. ② The shogun, *Tokugawa Iemochi* informed each
すぐに　通達した
domain of his decision on another *Choshu* Expedition
決定　長州再征
in 1866. ③ However, the *Satsuma* Domain, which the
shogunate counted on, refused to dispatch troops
～を頼りにした　拒否した　出兵する
because they had already formed an alliance with the
結んだ　同盟
Choshu Domain. ④ Nevertheless, the shogunate sent
それでも
about 100,000 soldiers to *Choshu*. ⑤ The *Choshu*
兵
Domain had the latest western guns which were
最新の洋式銃
purchased by using the name of the *Satsuma* Domain.
購入した　名義を利用して

⑥ The *Choshu* Domain fought back the shogunate troops and won a sweeping victory. ⑦ The failure of the Second War between the Shogunate and the *Choshu* Domain seriously dragged down the authority of the shogunate.

fought back 迎え撃った / won 得た / a sweeping victory 決定的な勝利 / the Second War between the Shogunate and the Choshu Domain 第二次幕長戦争 / dragged down 失墜させた / the authority 権威

和訳

①1864年の第一次幕長戦争では、長州藩がいち早く降伏したため、幕府は決定的なダメージを与えることはできませんでした。②1866年、将軍・徳川家茂は、長州再征を決定し、諸藩に通達しました。③しかし、幕府が頼りにしていた薩摩藩は、すでに薩長同盟を結んでいたため出兵を拒否しました。④それでも幕府は、約10万人もの兵を長州へと送り込みました。⑤長州藩は、薩摩藩の名義で購入した最新の洋式銃を所有していました。⑥長州藩は、幕府軍を迎え撃ち、ことごとく勝利をおさめました。⑦第二次幕長戦争の失敗は、幕府の権威をおおいに失墜(しっつい)させました。

23 The Last Shogun, Tokugawa Yoshinobu

最後の将軍・徳川慶喜

① *Hitotsubashi Yoshinobu* was born as the son (息子) of the *Mito* Domain leader *Tokugawa Nariaki*. ② *Yoshinobu* was adopted (養子となった) by the *Hitotsubashi* family (一橋家) and changed his surname (姓) to *Hitotsubashi*. ③ *Yoshinobu* was recommended (推薦された) as a successor (後継者として) of the 13th shogun (13代将軍), *Tokugawa Iesada*. ④ However, the successor was decided in favor of (～に賛成する) *Tokugawa Yoshitomi* by *Ii Naosuke*, the chief minister of the *Edo* shogunate (大老). ⑤ *Yoshitomi* became the 14th shogun, *Tokugawa Iemochi*. ⑥ After *Iemochi* died, *Yoshinobu* became the 15th shogun recommended by the senior councillors of the shogunate (老中). ⑦ At the time, the shogunate failed (失敗した) in the

Second War between the shoguante and the *Choshu*
第二次幕長戦争

Domain, and its power fell into decline. ⑧ Suggested
衰えていた　勧められた

by *Yamauchi Toyoshige*, *Yoshinobu* proposed the
申し入れた

Restoration of Imperial Rule to the Imperial Court.
大政奉還　朝廷

⑨ After the *Meiji* Restoration, he never appeared on
明治維新　姿を現わす

the front stage of politics.
表舞台　政治

和訳

①一橋慶喜は、水戸藩主・徳川斉昭(なりあき)の子として生まれました。②慶喜は一橋家に養子に入り、一橋姓を名乗りました。③13代将軍・徳川家定の後継者として推されました。④しかし、大老・井伊直弼によって家定の後継者は徳川慶福と決められました。⑤慶福は14代将軍・徳川家茂となりました。⑥家茂が亡くなると、慶喜は老中らに推されて15代将軍に就任しました。⑦当時、幕府は第二次幕長戦争に失敗し、衰(おとろ)えていました。⑧慶喜は、山内豊信の勧(すす)めにより、朝廷に大政奉還を申し入れました。⑨明治維新後は、政治の表舞台に出ることはありませんでした。

おさらいクイズ

【問題1】次の英語が表わす日本語を、あとのア〜ウから選びなさい。

① the Imperial Court
② Nationalistic Imperialism
③ the anti-shogunate movement

ア 尊王攘夷　イ 朝廷　ウ 倒幕運動

【問題2】次の日本語が表わす英語を、あとのア〜ウから選びなさい。

① 不平等条約改正
② 船中八策
③ 大政奉還

ア the Eight Outlines Laid Down on a Ship
イ the Restoration of Imperial Rule
ウ the amendment of unequal treaties

【問題3】次の英文の意味を、あとのア〜ウから選びなさい。

The reason for the formation of the *Roshi-gumi* by *Kiyokawa Hachiro* was to make use of them in the movement of expelling foreigners.

ア 清河八郎が浪士組を結成したのに、攘夷運動は収まりませんでした。
イ 清河八郎が浪士組を結成したので、攘夷運動が活発になりました。
ウ 清河八郎が浪士組を結成したのは、攘夷運動に利用するためでした。

【問題4】次の日本語を英文にしたものを、あとのア〜ウから選びなさい。

イギリスは報復として艦隊による薩摩藩への砲撃を行ないました。

ア England defended the *Satsuma* Domain by firing guns from the warships as an act of revenge.
イ England attacked the *Satsuma* Domain by firing guns from the warships as an act of colonization.
ウ England attacked the *Satsuma* Domain by firing guns from the warships as an act of revenge.

3章

戊辰(ぼしん)戦争

The Boshin War

【答え1】①イ　②ア　③ウ　【答え2】①ウ　②ア　③イ　【答え3】ウ
【答え4】ウ

24 The Restoration of Imperial Rule
大政奉還

① The *Satasuma* and *Choshu* Domains were secretly
もくろんでいた
planning to overthrow the shogunate by force. ② The
武力討幕
Tosa Domain intended to proceed with the reform
改革を進める
peacefully taking the stance of the union of the Imperial
立場をとる　公武合体
Court and the shogunate. ③ *Goto Shojiro* of the *Tosa*
Domain and *Sakamoto Ryoma* of *Kaientai* encouraged
働きかけた
the shogun, *Tokugawa Yoshinobu* to restore imperial
返還する
rule through *Yamauchi Toyoshige*, the former lord of
～を通じて　前土佐藩主
the *Tosa* Domain. ④ *Yoshinobu* proposed the
申し出た
Restoration of Imperial Rule to the Imperial Court on
大政奉還　朝廷
October 14, 1867. ⑤ *Yoshinobu* expected to remain a
期待した　とどまる
chairperson in the new regime, but things didn't go as
議長　新政権

he had anticipated. ⑥ Due to the realization of the
予想した ～のために 実現

Restoration of Imperial Rule, the *Satsuma* and the *Choshu* Domains lost their excuse of overthrowing the shogunate by force.
口実を失った

和訳

①薩摩藩や長州藩は武力討幕をもくろんでいました。②土佐藩は公武合体の立場をとり、平和的に改革を進めようとしていました。③土佐藩の後藤象二郎と海援隊の坂本龍馬は、前土佐藩主の山内豊信を通じて、将軍の徳川慶喜に大政奉還を行なうよう働きかけました。④慶喜は1867年10月14日、朝廷に大政奉還を申し出ました。⑤慶喜は、新政権下でも議長としてとどまることを期待していましたが、思惑どおりにはいきませんでした。⑥大政奉還が行なわれたことにより、薩摩藩や長州藩は武力討幕の口実を失うことになりました。

25 The Assassination of Sakamoto Ryoma

坂本龍馬の暗殺

① On November 15, 1867, *Sakamoto Ryoma* and *Nakaoka Shintaro* were in *Omiya*, which was *Ryoma's* boarding place (下宿先) in *Sanjyo-Kawaramachi*, *Kyoto*. ② At night, someone who wanted to see *Ryoma*, visited *Omiya*. ③ When the man who responded (取り次いだ) came down (下りてきた) from upstairs (2階), one of them killed the man. ④ They were the assassins (刺客) who came to kill *Ryoma*. ⑤ *Ryoma* heard the sound and said, "Don't make noise." (騒ぐな) ⑥ Because of this, the assassins found the room where *Ryoma* was. ⑦ The assassins came into the room and killed *Ryoma* and *Nakaoka*. ⑧ When the two didn't move any more, the assassins left (去った) the place.

⑨ Although the two victims regained consciousness,
けれども / 被害者 / 意識を取り戻した

Ryoma died soon after this. ⑩ *Nakaoka* died two days later. ⑪ The man who committed this assassination
実行した

was widely believed to be the guard force in *Kyoto*.
広く信じられている / 京都見廻組

和訳

①1867年11月15日、坂本龍馬と中岡慎太郎は、龍馬の下宿先である京都三条河原町(さんじょうかわらまち)の近江屋(おうみや)にいました。②夜になって、龍馬に面会したいという者たちが近江屋を訪れてきました。③取り次ぎをした男が2階から下りてくると、彼らの1人がその男を斬りました。④彼らは龍馬を暗殺にきた刺客(しかく)だったのです。⑤龍馬は物音に気づき、「騒ぐな」といいました。⑥この声によって、刺客たちは龍馬のいる部屋を探り当てました。⑦刺客たちはその部屋に乗り込み、龍馬と中岡を斬りました。⑧2人が動かなくなると、刺客たちは去りました。⑨2人は意識を取り戻しましたが、龍馬はまもなく亡くなりました。⑩中岡は2日後に亡くなりました。⑪暗殺の実行者は、京都見廻組(みまわりぐみ)の者であるとの説が有力です。

26 The Decree for the Restoration of Imperial Rule

王政復古の大号令

① On December 9, 1867, the warriors of the *Satsuma* and *Owari* Domains surrounded the Imperial Palace in *Kyoto*, and *Iwakura Tomomi*, a court noble, announced "the Decree for the Restoration of Imperial Rule" under the name of the Emperor. ② This was the coup by the group trying to overthrow the shogunate by force but lost the excuse to do so. ③ The shogunate, regent and chief advisor of the Emperor were abolished and three positions (*Sosai*, *Gijyo*, *Sanyo*) were established. ④ The new government which the Emperor was nucleus was founded, and the *Edo* shogunate which had lasted for 260 years ended. ⑤ In a meeting at the small Imperial

取り囲む　京都御所　公家　発令した　王政復古の大号令　〜の名において　天皇　クーデター　武力討幕　口実を失った　摂政　関白　廃止された　三職　設置された　新政権　中心　発足した　江戸幕府　続いた　小御所会議

Palace held from the evening on the same day, the treatment of *Tokugawa Yoshinobu* was violently discussed. ⑥ As a result, it was determined that *Yoshinobu* had to resign as Lord Keeper of the Privy Seal and return territory back to the *Tokugawas*.

処遇 / 激しく / 議論された / その結果 / 決定した / ～を辞職する / 内大臣 / 返上する / 領地

和訳

①1867年12月９日、薩摩藩や尾張（おわり）藩の兵士が京都御所の周囲を固め、公家の岩倉具視が天皇の名において「王政復古の大号令」を発表しました。②これは、大政奉還によって幕府を攻める口実を失った武力討幕派によるクーデターでした。③将軍・摂政（せっしょう）・関白（かんぱく）は廃止され、三職（さんしょく）（総裁（そうさい）・議定（ぎじょう）・参与（さんよ））が設置されました。④天皇を中心とする新政権が発足し、260年以上続いた江戸幕府はほろびました。⑤同日夕方から開かれた小御所会議（こごしょかいぎ）では、徳川慶喜の処遇について激しい論戦が行なわれました。⑥その結果、慶喜に対し、内大臣（ないだいじん）の職をやめさせて、徳川家の領地を朝廷に返上させることを決めました。

27

The Battle of Toba-Fushimi

鳥羽(とば)・伏見(ふしみ)の戦い

① After the coup of the Restoration of Imperial Rule, (王政復古のクーデター) *Tokugawa Yoshinobu*, last tried to reinstate (復権する) the position he had lost, and he was allowed (認められた) to join the new government (新政府). ② *Saigo Takamori*, who was in a group of the anti-shogunate by force (武力討幕), ordered (命令した) the members of the *Satsuma* Domain to commit (犯す) robbery (強盗) and arson (放火) in *Edo*. ③ *Yoshinobu* decided to subdue (討伐する) the *Satsuma* Domain and sent an army (軍隊) to *Kyoto*. ④ On January 3, 1868, the pro-shogunate army (旧幕府軍) and the new government army (新政府軍) fought at around *Toba-Fushimi* in the suburbs (近郊) of *Kyoto*. ⑤ When the red flags with a gold sun and a silver moon embroidered on each (錦の御旗), which represented (〜のしるしである)

the Imperial army, were hung up among the new
朝廷軍 掲げられた

government army, the situation suddenly turned to its
状況 ～に向かう

advantage. ⑥ *Yoshinobu* returned to *Edo* and the pro-
有利

shogunate army collapsed and lost completely.
崩れた 敗れた 完全に

和訳

①王政復古のクーデターのあと、失脚した徳川慶喜の復権が図(はか)られ、慶喜は新政府に加わることになりました。②武力討幕派の西郷隆盛は、薩摩藩士に命じて江戸で強盗や放火を行なわせました。③慶喜は薩摩藩討伐を決意し、京都へ大軍を送りました。④1868年１月３日、京都近郊の鳥羽・伏見付近で、旧幕府軍と新政府軍が衝突しました。⑤新政府軍に官軍(朝廷軍)のしるしである錦(にしき)の御旗(みはた)が掲げられると、戦況は一気に新政府軍のほうへ傾きました。⑥慶喜は江戸へ帰り、旧幕府軍は総崩れとなり、敗北しました。

28 The Five-Article Charter Oath
五箇条の誓文

① The *Meiji* Emperor (Emperor *Mutsuhito*) announced
明治天皇 発表した

"the Five-Article Charter Oath", which showed the
五箇条の誓文

basic policy of the *Meiji* government, in March of
基本方針

1868. ② It was established in the way that the Emperor
定められた

swore to god accompanying the nation. ③ *Kido*
神に誓う 国民を従えて

Takayoshi is said to have made the draft. ④ The Five-
～といわれている 下書きを書いた

Article Charter Oath consists of the following five
～から成っている 次の

statements. ⑤ We should have a wide range of

meetings, and all political affairs should be decided
万機(政治に関するすべての事柄)

based on public decision. ⑥ We should govern the
公論(国民の意見) 統治する

country by keeping order and uniting our hearts and
秩序 心をひとつにして

minds regardless of social class rank. ⑦ The common
～に関係なく 社会的地位 一般の人々

people, public servants or samurai and the general
官吏 庶民
public can seek their ambitions without losing their
遂げる 志
hopes or motivation. ⑧ We should abandon past evil
やる気 捨てる 過去の 悪い
customs and follow the universal truth. ⑨ We should
慣習 普遍の真理
seek our knowledge throughout the world and support
知識を求める ～のいたるところに
the foundation of our country centered around the
基礎 ～を中心とした
Emperor.

和訳

①1868年３月、明治天皇は、明治政府の基本方針である「五箇条の誓文」を発表しました。②天皇が国民を従えて、神に誓うという形式で定めたものでした。③木戸孝允が草案をつくったといわれています。④五箇条の誓文は、次の五箇条から成(な)っています。⑤広ク会議ヲ興(おこ)シ、万機公論(ばんきこうろん)ニ決スベシ。⑥上下(しょうか)心ヲ一(いつ)ニシテ、盛(さかん)ニ経綸(けいりん)ヲ行フベシ。⑦官武一途庶民(かんぶいつとしょみん)ニ至ル迄(まで)各(おのおの)其志(そのこころざし)ヲ遂(と)ゲ、人心ヲシテ倦(う)マザラシメン事ヲ要ス。⑧旧来(きゅうらい)ノ陋習(ろうしゅう)ヲ破リ、天地ノ公道(こうどう)ニ基(もとづ)クベシ。⑨智識(ちしき)ヲ世界ニ求メ、大(おおい)ニ皇基(こうき)ヲ振起(しんき)スベシ。

29 The Five Ban Notices

五榜(ごぼう)の掲示

① The *Meiji* government removed the notice board set up by the *Edo* shogunate and displayed "the Five Ban Notices" on the next day the Five-Article Charter Oath was announced. ② The first notice stated that people should follow Confucian morals. ③ The second one stated that people must not appeal directly in groups. ④ The third one stated that people were not allowed to believe in Christianity. ⑤ The fourth one stated that people were banned from attacking foreigners. ⑥ The fifth one stated that the public people must not run away from the country to go abroad. ⑦ The policy mentioned in the Five Ban

Meiji government: 明治政府 / removed: 取り外した / the notice board: 高札 / displayed: 掲げた / the Five Ban Notices: 五榜の掲示 / the Five-Article Charter Oath: 五箇条の誓文 / stated: はっきり述べた / follow: 従う / Confucian morals: 儒教道徳 / appeal directly in groups: 強訴する / Christianity: キリスト教 / the public people: 民衆 / run away: 脱走する / go abroad: 国外へ行く / policy: 政策 / mentioned: 挙げた

Notices was not so different from the policy of the *Edo*
違いはなかった
shogunate. ⑧ Later, several foreign countries protested
～に抗議した
against this and the fifth one was abolished. ⑨ The rest
廃止された　残りの
of the notices were all removed as well in later years.
通知　同様に

和訳

①五箇条の誓文が出された翌日、明治政府は江戸幕府の高札(こうさつ)を撤去し、「五榜の掲示」と呼ばれる５つの高札を新しく掲げました。②第一札では、儒教(じゅきょう)道徳を守るべきことなどが示されました。③第二札では、徒党(ととう)を組んで強訴(ごうそ)をしてはならないことなどが示されました。④第三札では、キリスト教を信じてはならないことが示されました。⑤第四札では、外国人に暴行を加えてはならないことが示されました。⑥第五札では、士民(しみん)が国外へ脱走してはならないことが示されました。⑦五榜の掲示によって示された民衆に対する政策は、江戸幕府の政策とあまり変わりませんでした。⑧その後、諸外国からの抗議を受け、第五札が取り外されました。⑨のちに残りの高札もすべて取り外されました。

30

The Bloodless Surrender of Edo Castle

江戸城の無血開城

I will leave this in your hands!
頼んだぞ！
勝海舟は、山岡鉄舟を使者に立て、会談を申し入れました。
Saigo...
西郷…
3月13日、勝海舟と西郷隆盛の会談が実現しました。
I request you to stop full-scale attack on Edo Castle.
江戸城総攻撃をやめてもらいたい。
If you surrender Edo Castle, it will be all right.
江戸城を明け渡すなら、よかとです。
勝海舟は、江戸城総攻撃中止を申し入れました。西郷隆盛は、江戸城明け渡しを条件に、総攻撃中止を約束しました。

31 The Boshin War and the Samurai Forces

戊辰戦争と彰義隊(しょうぎたい)

① The *Boshin* War (戊辰戦争) is a civil war (内戦) between the new government army (新政府軍) and the pro-shogunate army (旧幕府軍) that lasted from January of 1868 to May of 1869. ② The *Boshin* War started with the Battle of *Toba-Fushimi* (鳥羽・伏見の戦い) and ended with the victory (勝利) of the new government army in the War of *Hakodate* (箱館戦争). ③ One of the battles of the *Boshin* War was the *Ueno* War (上野戦争). ④ A samurai force called *Shogi-tai* (彰義隊) was formed (結成された) in order to (～するために) guard (警護する) *Tokugawa Yoshinobu*. ⑤ The *Shogi-tai* occupied (占拠した) *Kaneiji* Temple (寛永寺) in *Ueno* and intensified its confrontation with (～と対決を強めた) the new government army even after its Bloodless Surrender of *Edo* Castle (江戸城無血開城). ⑥ The new government planned to attack

Shogi-tai and sent *Oomura Masujiro* of the *Choshu* Domain as a commander. ⑦ The new government army started the attack on May 15, 1868 and the *Shogi-tai* was completely defeated.

指揮官

壊滅した

和訳

①戊辰戦争とは、1868年1月から翌年5月までの、新政府軍と旧幕府軍との戦いのことです。②戊辰戦争は、鳥羽・伏見の戦いから始まり、箱館戦争で新政府軍の勝利で終わりました。③戊辰戦争の戦いの1つが上野(うえの)戦争です。④徳川慶喜の身辺警護をするために彰義隊が結成されました。⑤彰義隊は江戸城無血開城後も上野の寛永寺を占拠し、新政府軍との対決姿勢を強めていました。⑥新政府は彰義隊の討伐を計画し、長州藩の大村益次郎(おおむらますじろう)を指揮官として派遣しました。⑦1868年5月15日、新政府軍が攻撃を開始、彰義隊は壊滅しました。

32

The Aizu War and Teenage Warriors
会津戦争と白虎隊（びゃっこたい）

① The *Aizu* Domain played a central role in the pro-
中心的な存在だった　旧幕府軍
shogunate army because the lord of the domain,
Matsudaira Katamori, had a position as a *Kyoto*
京都守護職
security guard. ② *Matsudaira Katamori* showed
従う姿勢を見せた
obedience to the new government, however, it
announced the order of attack. ③ The thirty-one
追討令
domains in the *Tohoku* and *Echigo* regions formed an
地方　結成した
alliance (the *Ouuetsu-Reppan* Alliance) in May of
同盟　奥羽越列藩同盟
1868 and took a stance of confrontation with the new
対決姿勢
government. ④ The new government army invaded
進攻した
Aizu-Wakamatsu Castle (*Tsuruga-jo*) to attack at the
〜の終わり
end of August. ⑤ The castle town was surrounded with
炎に包まれた

fire. ⑥ The *Byakko-tai*, which consisted of 20 teenaged
～から成り立った
boy warriors aged 15 to 17, thought *Aizu-Wakamatsu* Castle was surrendered by looking at the fire and
降参した
commited mass suicide. ⑦ The *Aizu* army held the
決意した 集団自決 籠城した
castle. ⑧ Finally, the *Aizu* army surrendered after its one-month long siege of the castle.
籠城戦

和訳

①会津藩は、藩主・松平容保(かたもり)が京都守護職についていたので、旧幕府軍の中心的な存在でした。②松平容保は、新政府に従う姿勢を示しましたが、新政府は追討令を出しました。③1868年５月、東北と越後(えちご)の31藩による同盟(奥羽越列藩同盟(おううえつれつぱんどうめい))が結成され、新政府との対決姿勢を強めました。④８月末、新政府軍は会津若松城(鶴ケ城(つるがじょう))まで進攻しました。⑤城下が炎に包まれました。⑥15～17歳の少年20人からなる白虎隊は、この炎を見て会津若松城が落城したと思い込み、集団自決しました。⑦会津軍は会津若松城に籠城(ろうじょう)しました。⑧会津軍は１カ月にわたる籠城戦の末、ついに降伏しました。

33 The Surrender of Star-shaped Castle

五稜郭（ごりょうかく）の陥落

① *Enomoto Takeaki*, who was the vice president of the
副総裁
pro-shogunate navy, escaped from *Edo* accompanying
旧幕府海軍　～から逃げた　引き連れて
eight shogunate warships in 1868. ② *Enomoto Takeaki*
軍艦
joined *Hijikata Toshizo* and the others from the group
of extreme warriors in *Sendai*. ③ The pro-shogunate
新選組　旧幕府軍
army led by *Enomoto Takeaki* landed in the *Ezo* region
蝦夷地
(*Hokkaido*). ④ The pro-shogunate army occupied
占拠した
Hakodate and established “the Republic of *Ezo*” in
打ち立てる　蝦夷共和国
which *Enomoto Takeaki* was the president. ⑤ The
総裁
new government army landed in the *Ezo* region in
1869. ⑥ The new government army invaded Star-
進攻した　五稜郭
shaped Castle, which was the base of *Enomoto's* army,

and started full-scale attack. ⑦ At that time, *Hijikata*
総攻撃

Toshizo was shot to death. ⑧ *Enomoto Takeaki*
銃弾を受けて死んだ

surrendered himself and Star-shaped Castle to the new
明け渡した

government army. ⑨ The *Boshin* War which lasted for
戊辰戦争 続いた

one year and five months ended by the victory of the new government army at the battle.

和訳

①1868年、旧幕府海軍副総裁だった榎本武揚(えのもとたけあき)は、幕府の軍艦８隻を引き連れて江戸を脱出しました。②榎本武揚は、仙台で新選組の土方歳三らと合流しました。③榎本武揚が率いる旧幕府軍は、蝦夷地(えぞち)(北海道)に上陸しました。④旧幕府軍は箱館を占拠し、榎本武揚を総裁として「蝦夷共和国」を打ち立てました。⑤1869年、新政府軍は蝦夷地に上陸しました。⑥新政府軍は、榎本軍の拠点である五稜郭に進攻し、総攻撃を加えました。⑦この時、土方歳三は銃弾を受けて戦死しました。⑧榎本武揚は降伏し、五稜郭を明け渡しました。⑨新政府軍がこの戦いで勝利を収めたことで、１年５カ月にわたった戊辰戦争が終結しました。

34 Reform Riots and the 'Happy-Go-Lucky' Protest Movement

世直し一揆（いっき）とええじゃないか騒動

① Farmer riots and acts of destruction called "Reform
百姓一揆　打ちこわし　世直し一揆

Riots" occurred frequently in 1866. ② This was due to
多発した

crop failure that lasted for several years or prices that
凶作　数年続いた　物価の激しい上昇

rose sharply under the effect of opening the country.
影響　開国

③ Another reason for these riots was that the taxes
一揆

called *Nengu* had been raised because of the Second
第二次幕長戦争

War between the Shogunate and the *Choshu* Domain.

④ The riots happened in *Osaka* and *Edo* where rice
米屋

stores and pawnshops were broken into demanding for
質屋　襲われた　要求

discounts on rice. ⑤ In 1867, the people dancing in
安売り

groups and shouting "Happy time is coming" appeared
ええじゃないか　発生した

throughout the country. ⑥ One of the causes was the
原因

rumor that the religious paper of *Ise* Shrine fell down
うわさ　お札　伊勢神宮

from the sky. ⑦ The 'Happy-Go-Lucky' Protest Movement occurred in many places mainly in the *Tokai* and *Kinki* areas and it lasted until around April the following year.
ええじゃないか騒動　翌年

和訳

①1866年、「世直し一揆」と呼ばれる百姓一揆や打ちこわしが多発しました。②数年にわたる凶作（きょうさく）や、開国の影響で物価が激しく上昇したことが原因といわれています。③第二次幕長戦争を理由に年貢が増えたことも世直し一揆が増えた原因でした。④大坂や江戸で打ちこわしが発生し、米の安売りを要求して、米屋や質屋が襲われました。⑤1867年には、「ええじゃないか」といいながら、集団で踊る人々の群れが各地で発生しました。⑥伊勢（いせ）神宮のお札が降ってきたといううわさがきっかけとなったといわれています。⑦ええじゃないか騒動は、東海や近畿を中心として各地で起こり、翌年の４月頃まで続きました。

35 The Order of Separating Shintoism and Buddhism and the Anti-Buddhist Movement

神仏分離令と廃仏毀釈（はいぶつきしゃく）

① The *Meiji* government issued the Order of Separating Shintoism and Buddhism in 1868 in order to promote the policy of establishing Shintoism as the national religion. ② The order was a law which meant to remove things related to Buddhism from shrines. ③ By this order, worshipping Buddha as God was banned in shrines, and hanging temple bells and little bells called *Waniguchi* were ordered to be removed. ④ In Japan, there had been a custom of the syncretic fusion of Shintoism and Buddhism since many years ago. ⑤ The *Meiji* government tried to clearly separate Shintoism and Buddhism under this order. ⑥ The order led to a

Meiji government：明治政府　issued：発布した　the Order of Separating Shintoism and Buddhism：神仏分離令　promote the policy：政策を進める　Shintoism：神道　the national religion：国教　a law：法律　remove：取り除く　related to：〜に関係する　Buddhism：仏教　shrines：神社　worshipping Buddha as God：仏像を崇めること　was banned：禁止された　hanging temple bells：梵鐘　the syncretic fusion of Shintoism and Buddhism：神仏習合　clearly separate：明確に区別する　led to：〜を誘発した

lot of anti-Buddhist movements everywhere in the
廃仏毀釈

country. ⑦ The anti-Buddhist movement was intended to exclude Buddhism. ⑧ By these movements, Buddhist practices, the images of Buddha and sutras were thrown away or destroyed around the country.

~を意図した 排除する 仏道 仏像 経文 破棄された 破壊された

和訳

①明治政府は、神道（しんとう）を国教化する政策を進めるために1868年、神仏分離令を発布しました。②神仏分離令とは、神社から仏教的なものを取り除くよう決めた法律でした。③神仏分離令によって、神社では、仏像を神体とすることが禁止され、梵鐘（ぼんしょう）や鰐口（わにぐち）を取り外すよう求められました。④日本では昔から神仏習合（しんぶつしゅうごう）が行なわれてきました。⑤明治政府は、神仏分離令によって、神道と仏教を明確に区別しようとしたのです。⑥神仏分離令がきっかけとなって、全国各地で廃仏毀釈が行なわれました。⑦廃仏毀釈とは、仏教を排斥（はいせき）しようとする運動のことです。⑧廃仏毀釈によって仏像、経文（きょうもん）などが各地で破棄・破壊されました。

36 Three New Religions at the End of the Shogunate

幕末三大新宗教

① *Tenri-kyo*, *Kurozumi-kyo* and *Konko-kyo* created in the end of the shogunate were new sects of Shintoism.
幕末 / 神道系の新宗教

② *Tenri-kyo* was founded by a farmer's housewife,
創始された

Nakayama Miki in *Yamato* (now *Nara* Prefecture).

③ *Kurozumi-kyo* was created by *Kurozumi Munetada*, a *Negi* (Shintoism priest) in *Bizen* (now *Okayama*
神職の職名

Prefecture). ④ *Konko-kyo* was founded by a farmer, *Akazawa Bunji* in *Bitchu* (now *Okayama* Prefecture).

⑤ These new religions were spread among the people
広まった / 民衆

who sought for relief during the chaos in the end of the
救いを求める / 混乱期

shogunate. ⑥ In the *Meiji* period, they became one sect
明治時代 / ～の一派

of *Kyoha Shinto*. ⑦ *Kyoha Shinto* is a religious group
宗教団体

of the Shintoism sects authorized by the government
神道系 公認された
during the *Meiji* period.

和訳

①天理教・黒住教・金光教は、幕末に創始された神道系の新宗教です。②天理教は、農家の主婦であった中山みきが大和(現・奈良県)で創始しました。③黒住教は、禰宜(神職の職名)の黒住宗忠が備前(現・岡山県)で創始しました。④金光教は、農民の赤沢文治が備中(現・岡山県)で創始しました。⑤これらの新宗教は、幕末の混乱期に救いを求める民衆のあいだに広まっていきました。⑥明治時代になると、これらの新宗教は、教派神道の一派となりました。⑦教派神道とは、明治時代に政府から公認された神道系の宗教団体のことをいいます。

おさらいクイズ

【問題1】次の日本語が表わす英語を、あとのア〜ウから選びなさい。

① 王政復古
② 旧幕府軍
③ ええじゃないか

ア the pro-shogunate army
イ happy time is coming
ウ the restoration of Imperial Rule

【問題2】次の英語が表わす日本語を、あとのア〜ウから選びなさい。

① assassination
② coup
③ regime

ア 暗殺　イ クーデター　ウ 政権

【問題3】次の英文の意味を、あとのア〜ウから選びなさい。

The *Boshin* War started with the Battle of *Toba-Fushimi* and ended with the victory of the new government army in the War of *Hakodate*.

ア 戊辰戦争は、鳥羽・伏見の戦いから始まり、箱館戦争で新政府軍の勝利で終わりました。
イ 戊辰戦争は、箱館戦争から始まり、鳥羽・伏見の戦いで新政府軍の勝利で終わりました。
ウ 戊辰戦争は、鳥羽・伏見の戦いから始まり、箱館戦争で旧幕府軍の勝利で終わりました。

【問題4】次の英文の(　)にあてはまる1語を書きなさい。

Enomoto Takeaki (　　) himself and Star-shaped Castle to the new government army.
榎本武揚は新政府軍に降伏し、五稜郭を明け渡しました。

4章
明治維新
The Meiji Restoration

【答え1】①ウ　②ア　③イ　【答え2】①ア　②イ　③ウ　【答え3】ア
【答え4】surrendered

37 Emperor Mutsuhito
明治天皇

① Emperor *Komei* passed away on December 25,
崩御した

1866. ② The Royal Prince, *Mutsuhito*, succeeded to
親王 ～を継承した

the throne and became Emperor *Mutsuhito* on January
皇位 明治天皇

9, 1867. ③ At that time, he was only 16 years old.

④ This was the emperor who succeeded to the throne

during the chaos in the end of the shogunate. ⑤ On
動乱期に 幕末

October 14th in the same year, shogun, *Tokugawa*

Yoshinobu proposed the Restoration of Imperial Rule
申し入れをした 大政奉還

and the emperor accepted this. ⑥ In December of the
受け入れた

same year, he issued the Decree for the Restoration of
公布した 王政復古の大号令

Imperial Rule and the *Meiji* government was

established. ⑦ In 1868, the name *Edo* was changed to
誕生した

Tokyo and Emperor *Mutsuhito* moved from *Kyoto* to *Tokyo*. ⑧ Emperor *Mutsuhito* tackled various reforms.
取り組んだ　改革
⑨ He issued the Constitution of the Empire of Japan
大日本帝国憲法
on February 11, 1889 and he became a monarch of a
君主
modern nation which had both a constitution and
憲法
a parliament, which was the first in Asia.
議会

和訳

①1866年12月25日、孝明天皇が崩御（ほうぎょ）しました。②翌1867年1月9日、睦仁（むつひと）親王が皇位を継承し、明治天皇となりました。③この時、わずか満16歳でした。④幕末の動乱期に誕生した天皇でした。⑤同年10月14日、将軍・徳川慶喜から大政奉還の申し入れがあり、明治天皇はこれを受け入れました。⑥同年12月、王政復古の大号令を発令し、新政府が誕生しました。⑦1868年、江戸は東京と改められ、明治天皇は京都から東京へ移りました。⑧明治天皇はさまざまな改革に取り組みました。⑨1889年2月11日に大日本帝国憲法を発布、アジアで初の憲法と議会を持つ近代国家の君主となったのです。

38 Three Outstanding Heroes of the Restoration and Genkun

維新の三傑(さんけつ)と元勲(げんくん)

① The three people of distinguished achievements (功績のある) from the overthrow of the shogunate (討幕) to the *Meiji* Restoration (明治維新), *Saigo Takamori*, *Okubo Toshimichi* and *Kido Takayoshi* are called "the Three Outstanding Heroes of the Restoration" (維新の三傑). ② *Saigo Takamori* had a conference (会談を行なった) with *Katsu Kaishu* and realized (実現させた) the Bloodless Surrender of *Edo* Castle (江戸城無血開城). ③ He insisted on (〜を主張した) the Policy of Conquering Korea (征韓論), however, he lost the political strife (政争) and left the government. ④ *Okubo Toshimichi* and *Kido Takayoshi* played a central role (中心的な役割を果たした) in the new *Meiji* government and carried out reforms (改革を行なった) like the Restoration of Domain Lands and Public Generals (版籍奉還),

and the Abolition of Domains and the Establishment
廃藩置県
of Prefectures. ⑤ In addition to the three people, the
〜に加えて
court nobles, *Sanjo Sanetomi* and *Iwakura Tomoni*,
公家
Itagaki Taisuke of the *Tosa* Domain, *Goto Shojiro* and *Eto Shinpei* of the *Saga* Domain and others with distinguished achievements during the *Meiji* Restoration, were called "*Genkun*".
元勲

和訳

①討幕から明治維新に特別功績のあった、西郷隆盛・大久保利通（おおくぼとしみち）・木戸孝允の３人を「維新の三傑」と呼びます。②西郷隆盛は、勝海舟と会談を行なって江戸城無血開城を実現させました。③明治政府では征韓論（せいかんろん）を主張し、政争に敗れ、政府を去りました。④大久保利通や木戸孝允は、明治新政府で中心的な役割を果たし、版籍奉還（はんせきほうかん）や廃藩置県（はいはんちけん）などの改革を行ないました。⑤３人のほか、公家出身の三条実美（さんじょうさねとみ）、岩倉具視、土佐藩出身の板垣退助、後藤象二郎、佐賀藩出身の江藤新平（えとうしんぺい）ら、明治維新に功績のあった人々を「元勲」と呼びます。

39 The Relocation of the Capital to Tokyo and the Change of the Era Name to Meiji

東京遷都と明治改元

① The new government moved the capital to *Edo* in order to regenerate the public mind. ② The name *Edo* was changed to "*Tokyo*". ③ *Tokyo* meant "eastern capital" as opposed to *Kyoto* in the west. ④ Emperor *Mutsuhito* moved from *Kyoto* to *Tokyo* and the government institution was moved as well in 1868. ⑤ The era name was also changed in order to announce to the public that the new era had come. ⑥ The era name, *Meiji*, was decided. ⑦ Era names had often been changed in the time of disaster during the reign of the emperor previously. ⑧ However, the Emperor announced "an imperial edict indicating that one reign

new government 新政府 / the capital 首都 / in order to 〜するために / regenerate 一新する / as opposed to 〜に対して / government institution 政府機関 / era name 元号 / in order to 〜するために / the new era had come 新しい時代になった / in the time of 〜の時 / disaster 災害 / during the reign of the emperor 天皇の在位中 / an imperial edict indicating that one reign 一世一元の詔

should have one Era name" and it was decided that each Emperor would have only one Era name after *Meiji.*

和訳

①新政府は、人心(じんしん)を一新するために都を江戸に移しました。②江戸は「東京」と改称されました。③東京とは、京都に対する「東(ひがし)の京(みやこ)」という意味でした。④1868年、明治天皇は京都から東京に移り、政府の機関も東京に移りました。⑤新しい時代になったことを広く国民に示すために元号(げんごう)を変えることになりました。⑥元号は「明治」と決められました。⑦それまで元号は、災害があった時など、天皇の在位中にもしばしば変更されてきました。⑧しかし、「一世一元(いっせいいちげん)の詔(みことのり)」が出され、明治以降は天皇１人に対して１つの元号とすることが定められました。

40 The Restoration of Domain Lands and Public Generals

はんせきほうかん
版籍奉還

① The new *Meiji* government set the aim of making
目指した
Japan strong enough to compete with western countries.
～に十分な ～と肩を並べる
② *Kido Takayoshi* of the *Choshu* Domain and *Okubo Toshimichi* of the *Satsuma* Domain played a key role in
中心的な役割をした
planning "the Restoration of Domain Lands and Public
版籍奉還
Generals". ③ This is the reform of returning domain
改革 返還 領地
lands and public generals to the Emperor. ④ The
領民
Restoration of Domain Lands and Public Generals was ordered in 1869, and lands and public generals in
命令された
the nation were all returned to the government. ⑤ The government still appointed the same domain lords as
指名した 藩主
governors of former domains and allowed them to
知藩事（地方官）

engage in local politics of the former domains even
～に携わる　地方政治　旧領地

after the Restoration of Domain Lands and Public Generals. ⑥ However, the governors still had the authority of military affairs and tax collection as before,
権限　軍事　徴税

so the reform was not enough.
十分ではなかった

和訳

①明治政府は、日本を欧米諸国と肩を並べる強い国にすることを目指しました。②長州藩出身の木戸孝允、薩摩藩出身の大久保利通が中心となって「版籍奉還」を画策(かくさく)しました。③これは、それまで各藩の藩主が支配していた版（領地）と籍（領民）を天皇に返還させる改革です。④1869年、版籍奉還が命じられ、全国の領地と領民は政府のもとに置かれました。⑤政府は、版籍奉還後も藩主をそのまま知藩事(ちはんじ)（地方官）に任命し、旧領地の政治を任(まか)せました。⑥しかし、軍事や徴税(ちょうぜい)の権限などは以前と変わらず知藩事が握ったため、十分な改革にはなりませんでした。

41 The Abolition of Domains and the Establishment of Prefectures

廃藩置県（はいはんちけん）

① The *Meiji* government needed to secure financial
確保する　財源
resources and an army. ② Territory and public generals
領地　人民
were put under the charge of the Emperor due to the
〜のもとに置かれた　管理　〜のために
Restoration of Domain Lands and Public Generals.
版籍奉還
③ However, the former feudal lords still ruled each
旧藩主　治めた
domain as governors and had the authority of tax
知藩事　権限　徴税
collection as well as the army. ④ The government
〜と同様に
dismissed all the domain governors and settled them in
罷免した　移住させた
Tokyo. ⑤ The domains were abolished and the country
藩　廃止された
was divided into three urban prefectures and three
〜に分割された　府
hundred and two prefectures, and the government let
県　させた
the prefectural governors, who were elected and sent
府知事・県知事　選ばれた　送られた

out from the central areas, rule them. ⑥ This is the Abolition of Domains and the Establishment of Prefectures. ⑦ The rule by feudal lords had completely disappeared and the *Meiji* government was centralized.

中央 / 廃藩置県 / 大名 / 完全に / 消滅した / 中央集権化された

和訳

①明治政府は、財源と軍隊を確保する必要がありました。②版籍奉還によって、領地と人民は天皇のものとなりました。③しかし、旧藩主が知藩事として従来のまま各藩を治めており、徴税と軍事の権限を握っていました。④政府は、知藩事をすべて罷免（ひめん）して東京へ移住させました。⑤藩を廃止して、全国を３府302県に分け、政府が選んだ県知事を中央から派遣して治めさせました。⑥これが廃藩置県です。⑦大名による支配は完全になくなり、明治政府による中央集権が確立しました。

42 The Centralized Nation and the Central Government System
中央集権国家と太政官（だじょうかん）制度

① The *Meiji* government built (築いた) the centralized nation (中央集権国家) centering around the Emperor in order to (〜のために) establish (設立) the modern nation (近代国家) which could equally compete with western countries. ② In order to achieve (実現する) this, the organization (組織) of the central government (中央政府) was reinforced (強化された). ③ It announced (公布した) the law related to political organization (政体書) and allowed (認めた) national power to center (集中する) to the central government (太政官（中央政府）). ④ This administrative system (行政制度) is "the Central Government System" (太政官制度). ⑤ The system was established by *Okubo Toshimichi*, *Kido Takayoshi*, *Goto Shojiro* and the others from the four domains (*Satsuma*, *Choshu*, *Tosa*, *Hizen*) called *Sacchodohi* (薩長土肥) with reference to (〜にならって) the systems

of western countries. ⑥ It adopted the separation of
採用した　独立

legislative, executive and judicial powers. ⑦ *Giseikan*
立法　行政　司法

was in charge of legislative power, *Gyoseikan* was
～を担当した　立法

executive, and *Keihokan* was judiciary. ⑧ The central
司法

government system had lasted going through some
続いた

changes until the cabinet system started in 1885.
変化　内閣制度

和訳

①明治政府は、天皇を中心とする中央集権体制で欧米諸国と対等な近代国家をつくることを目指しました。②それを実現するために中央政府の組織を整備しました。③政体書（せいたいしょ）（政治組織を定めた法律）を公布し、国家権力を太政官（中央政府）に集中させました。④この行政制度が「太政官制度」です。⑤この制度は、欧米の制度にならって、大久保利通や木戸孝允、後藤象二郎ら薩長土肥（さっちょうどひ）の出身者によってつくられました。⑥立法・行政・司法の三権分立制も取り入れられました。⑦立法は議政官（ぎせいかん）、行政は行政官、司法は刑法官（けいほうかん）が担当しました。⑧太政官制度は、数度の変遷（へんせん）を経て、1885年に内閣制度が発足（ほっそく）するまで続きました。

43 The Iwakura Mission in Western Countries

岩倉米欧(いわくらべいおう)使節団

Oh my!
It moved!
わー！ 動いた！
産業革命を成し遂げたイギリスでは驚きの連続でした。
To maintain our independence, we need wealth and military strength!
独立を保つには、富国強兵だ！
ドイツでは、首相・ビスマルクの演説に感銘を受けました。
We shouldn't be colonized by any countries!
日本を植民地にしてはならない！
帰路、目にしたのは欧米の植民地となったアジアの国々でした。
We will quickly catch up with western countries!
早く欧米に追いつくぞ！
帰国した人々は、日本を強い国家にすることを誓いました。

44 The Equality of People from Four Feudal Classes

四民平等

① The *Meiji* government worked on the abolition of
～に取り組んだ 廃止

the feudal social class system. ② Feudal lords and
封建的な身分制度 大名

court nobles were categorized into noblemen, warriors
公家 ～に分類された 華族 武士

were warrior class, farmers, artisans and merchants
士族 農民 工民 商民

were commoners. ③ The government announced a
平民 公布した

liberation law and the people who were discriminated
解放令 差別されてきた

against till then, were classified as commoners.
それまで

④ This policy is called "the Equality of People from
四民平等

Four Feudal Classes". ⑤ Even though the feudal class
身分制度

system was abolished, discrimination actually lasted
差別 現実に 続いた

in many aspects of life such as residence, marriage,
生活のさまざまな面で 居住

employment and so forth, therefore, total equality could
就職 そのために 完全な四民平等

not be realized（実現する）. ⑥ The government established the family registration law（戸籍法） in 1871 and created the nation wide（全国的な） family register（戸籍） the following year（翌年）. ⑦ This is called “*Jinshin-koseki*”. ⑧ The government got hold of（～を掌握した） all nations and completed the foundation（基礎を築いた） of conscription（徴兵） and tax payment（納税） through the creation（作成） of the family register.

和訳

①明治政府は、封建（ほうけん）的な身分制度の廃止に取り組みました。②大名と公家を華族（かぞく）に、武士を士族（しぞく）、農工商民を平民（へいみん）としました。③解放令を出し、それまで差別されていた人々を、平民に組み込みました。④これらの政策を「四民平等」といいます。⑤身分制度が廃止されても、実際には居住・結婚・就職などさまざまな面で差別は続き、完全な四民平等は実現できませんでした。⑥政府は、1871年に戸籍（こせき）法を制定し、翌年に全国的な戸籍をつくりました。⑦これを「壬申（じんしん）戸籍」といいます。⑧戸籍の作成により、政府はすべての国民を掌握（しょうあく）し、徴兵（ちょうへい）や納税の基礎ができあがりました。

45 The Abolition of Payment for Noblemen and the Warrior Class, and the Sword Prohibition Edict

秩禄処分と廃刀令

(ちつろく はいとうれい)

① The *Meiji* government paid salaries called "*Chitsuroku*" to the warrior class and noblemen. ② The people in the warrior class who performed greatly in the Restoration of Imperial Rule were paid reward money called *Syotenroku*. ③ These spendings pressed the finance of the government. ④ The government abolished *Chitsuroku* by providing bonds with interest to the warrior class. ⑤ This is called "the Abolition of Payment". ⑥ There were some warrior class people who started unfamiliar business using these bonds as starting funds but failed, and this was called "the Warriors' Way of Businesses". ⑦ Many warrior class

salaries：給料
the warrior class：士族
noblemen：華族
performed greatly：功績があった
the Restoration of Imperial Rule：王政復古
reward money：報奨金
spendings：支出
pressed the finance：財政を圧迫した
abolished：廃止した
bonds with interest：利子つきの公債
the Abolition of Payment：秩禄処分
unfamiliar business：慣れない商売
starting funds：元手として
the Warriors' Way of Businesses：士族の商法

went bankrupt. ⑧ The *Meiji* government issued "the
没落した

Sword Prohibition Edict" and abolished the possession
廃刀令 刀の所持

of swords by people with the exception of military men
～以外の 軍人

and policemen. ⑨ The privileges of the warrior class,
特権

were all removed due to the Abolition of Payment and
すべて奪われた

the Sword Prohibition Edict.

和訳

①明治政府は、士族や華族に「秩禄」と呼ばれる給与を支払っていました。②王政復古に功績があった士族らには、報奨金(ほうしょうきん)として賞典禄(しょうてんろく)を支払っていました。③これらの支出は、政府の財政を圧迫していました。④政府は利子(りし)つきの公債(こうさい)を士族に与えて秩禄の支払いを廃止しました。⑤これを「秩禄処分」といいます。⑥公債をもとに慣れない商売に手を出し、失敗した士族もおり、「士族の商法」といわれました。⑦多くの士族は没落していきました。⑧明治政府は「廃刀令」を出し、軍人と警察官以外が刀を持つことを廃止しました。⑨秩禄処分と廃刀令によって、士族の特権はすべて奪われました。

46 The Rebellion of Dissatisfied People of Warrior Class

不平士族の反乱

① In the *Edo* period, warriors were privileged.
特権が与えられていた

② However, they were deprived of their privileges and
～を奪われた 特権

were getting poor due to the Equality of People from
貧困になっていった 四民平等

Four Feudal Classes, the Sword Prohibition Edict and
廃刀令

the Abolition of Payment which the *Meiji* government
秩禄処分

had carried out. ③ The dissatisfied warriors raised riots
実施した 不平を持った武士 反乱を起こした

everywhere in the nation. ④ The former *Saga* Domain
旧佐賀藩

members led by *Eto Shinpei* burnt down the *Saga*
～に率いられた 焼き払った 佐賀県庁

prefectural office in 1874. ⑤ This is called "the *Saga*
佐賀の乱

Rebellion". ⑥ The *Keishin* group from the former
敬神党

Kumamoto Domain roused themselves to action in
決起した

1876. ⑦ This is called "the *Shinpuren* Rebellion".

⑧ The former *Akizuki* Domain members raised an army (挙兵した) in the same year and the former *Hagi* Domain members also rose in revolt (蜂起した). ⑨ These are “the *Akizuki* Rebellion” and “the *Hagi* Rebellion”. ⑩ These rebellions were all suppressed (すべて鎮圧された) by the army dispatched (派遣された) from the government.

和訳

①江戸時代、武士は特権階級でした。②しかし、明治政府が実施した四民平等、廃刀令、秩禄処分などの政策によって、武士は特権を奪われ、経済的にも苦しくなっていきました。③不平士族は各地で反乱を起こしました。④1874年、江藤新平を中心に旧佐賀藩士が佐賀県庁を焼き払いました。⑤これを「佐賀の乱」といいます。⑥1876年には、旧熊本(くまもと)藩の敬神党(けいしんとう)が決起しました。⑦これを「神風連(しんぷうれん)の乱」といいます。⑧同年、秋月(あきづき)藩の旧藩士が挙兵し、旧萩(はぎ)藩の藩士も蜂起(ほうき)しました。⑨これらを「秋月の乱」「萩の乱」といいます。⑩これらの反乱は、政府に派遣された軍によってすべて鎮圧されました。

47

The Policy of Conquering Korea

征韓論（せいかんろん）

① The *Meiji* government hoped for diplomatic relations with Korea. ② However, Korea was under the Isolation Policy, so it didn't accept the negotiation. ③ Within the government, *Saigo Takamori* and *Itagaki Taisuke* insisted on "the Policy of Conquering Korea", making Korea open its country by force. ④ The government decided to send *Saigo Takamori* as an envoy to Korea. ⑤ However, *Okubo Toshimichi* and *Kido Takayoshi* who returned from their visit to western countries, opposed the policy. ⑥ *Okubo* and the others insisted that promoting domestic modernization was the first priority. ⑦ The dispatch of *Saigo* was

hoped for：～を望んだ　diplomatic relations：国交　the Isolation Policy：鎖国　accept：応じる　the negotiation：交渉　Within：～の中で　insisted on：～を主張した　the Policy of Conquering Korea：征韓論　open its country：開国する　by force：武力で　decided：決定した　an envoy：使節　opposed：反対した　insisted：主張した　promoting：進めること　domestic modernization：国内の近代化　the first priority：最優先事項　The dispatch：派遣

cancelled because *Okubo's* opinion was accepted.
中止された　受け入れられた

⑧ *Saigo Takamori* and *Itagaki Taisuke* left the government after they were defeated in the dispute over Korea.
去った　敗れた　論争

和訳

①明治政府は、朝鮮(ちょうせん)との国交を望んでいました。②しかし、朝鮮は鎖国していたため、交渉に応じませんでした。③西郷隆盛や板垣退助らは、政府内で武力によって朝鮮を開国させようという「征韓論」を主張しました。④政府は西郷隆盛を使節として朝鮮に派遣(はけん)することを決めました。⑤しかし、欧米視察から帰ってきた大久保利通や木戸孝允らは、征韓論に反対しました。⑥大久保らは、まず国内の近代化を進めることが優先だと主張したのです。⑦大久保らの意見が通り、西郷の派遣は中止されました。⑧朝鮮をめぐる論争に敗れた西郷隆盛や板垣退助らは政府を去りました。

48 The Seinan War
西南戦争

① *Saigo Takamori* was defeated in the dispute over the Policy of Conquering Korea and returned to his hometown, *Kagoshima*. ② Many warriors adoring *Saigo Takamori* gathered in *Kagoshima*. ③ *Saigo Takamori* couldn't suppress the dissatisfaction of his fellows and he raised an army relenting to the pressure from warriors in 1877. ④ This riot is called "the *Seinan* War". ⑤ *Saigo's* army attacked *Kumamoto* Castle, but it couldn't defeat it, and instead, the government army entered the castle and chased them up. ⑥ Although *Saigo's* army fought severely at *Tabaruzaka* and *Yamaga*, it kept getting defeated. ⑦ *Saigo's* army

敗れた　論争　征韓論　故郷　慕う　集まった　不満を抑える　同志　挙兵した　押し立てられて　反乱　西南戦争　攻めた　その代わりに　入城した　～を追い詰めた　けれども　激闘した　敗北を重ねた

retreated to *Kagoshima* and the war ended with *Saigo's*
～へ撤退した

suicide. ⑧ The *Seinan* War was the biggest civil war
自刃(自殺) 内戦

in Japanese history with more than 6,000 deaths.

和訳

①西郷隆盛は、征韓論をめぐる政争に敗れ、故郷の鹿児島に戻りました。②西郷隆盛を慕(した)う多くの士族が鹿児島に集まりました。③西郷隆盛は彼らの不満を抑えきれず、1877年、士族らに押し立てられて挙兵しました。④この反乱を「西南戦争」といいます。⑤西郷軍は、熊本城を攻めましたが落とせず、政府軍が入城して追い詰められました。⑥西郷軍は、田原坂(たばるざか)や山鹿(やまが)などで激闘しましたが敗北を重ねました。⑦西郷軍は鹿児島に撤退し、西郷の自刃(じじん)によって終戦しました。⑧西南戦争は、戦死者6000人を超える日本史上最大の内乱でした。

49 The Assassination of Okubo Toshimichi

大久保利通(おおくぼとしみち)の暗殺

① On May 14, 1878, *Okubo Toshimichi* got on a horse-
～に乗った 馬車
drawn carriage to leave his mansion in *Urakasumigaseki*.
屋敷を出る
② When the carriage passed through *Kioi* slope to the
紀尾井坂
gate of *Akasaka* and reached the *Mibu* estate, six
壬生邸
assassins attacked him. ③ *Shimada Ichiro* and *Cho*
刺客
Tsurahide who were the former *Kaga* Domain members,
旧加賀藩
stopped the carriage and slashed the horse's foot.
止めた 斬った
④ *Okubo Toshimichi* shouted "What insolent fellows
無礼者
you are!" ⑤ However, he was slashed from the front
切りつけられた 前後から
and behind, and died. ⑥ He was 49 years old at death.

⑦ The assassins blamed the autocracy of the domain
非難した 専制政治 薩長藩閥
groups of *Saccho*, the waste of national expenses and
浪費 国費

the corruption of government officials and used them
腐敗　政府官吏

as excuses for the assassination. ⑧ This incident is
理由として　事件

also called "the *Kioizaka* Incident". ⑨ After the death
紀尾井坂の変

of *Okubo*, political leadership shifted to *Ito Hirobumi*
政治の主導権　～に移った

of the *Choshu* Domain.

和訳

①1878年５月14日、大久保利通は馬車に乗り、裏霞ヶ関(うらかすみがせき)の屋敷を出ました。②馬車が紀尾井坂(きおいざか)から赤坂御門(あかさかごもん)の前を通り、壬生邸(みぶてい)にさしかかった頃、６人の刺客が襲いかかりました。③旧加賀(かが)藩士の島田一郎(しまだいちろう)、長連豪(ちょうつらひで)らは大久保利通の馬車を止め、馬の脚を斬りました。④大久保は、「無礼者」と一喝しました。⑤しかし、前後から刃(やいば)を受け、命を落としました。⑥享年49歳でした。⑦犯人らは、薩長藩閥の専制政治や、国費の浪費、政府官吏(かんり)の私利私欲などを暗殺理由として挙げました。⑧大久保利通暗殺事件を「紀尾井坂の変」ともいいます。⑨大久保亡きあと、政治の主導権は伊藤博文らの長州閥に移りました。

おさらいクイズ

【問題1】次の英語が表わす日本語を、あとのア～ウから選びなさい。

① the prefectural governors
② the *Meiji* Restoration
③ the Policy of Conquering Korea

ア 明治維新　　イ 県知事　　ウ 征韓論

【問題2】次の日本語が表わす英語を、あとのア～ウから選びなさい。

① 版籍奉還
② 四民平等
③ 廃藩置県

ア the Equality of People from Four Feudal Classes
イ the Restoration of Domain Lands and Public Generals
ウ the Abolition of Domains and the Establishment of Prefectures

【問題3】次の英文の意味を、あとのア～ウから選びなさい。

After the death of *Okubo*, political leadership shifted to *Ito Hirobumi* of the *Choshu* Domain.

ア 伊藤博文亡きあと、政治の主導権は大久保ら長州閥に移りました。
イ 大久保、伊藤博文亡きあと、政治の主導権は長州閥に移りました。
ウ 大久保亡きあと、政治の主導権は伊藤博文ら長州閥に移りました。

【問題4】次の英文の(　)にあてはまる1語を書きなさい。

These rebellions were all suppressed by the (　　) dispatched from the government.
これらの反乱は、政府によって派遣された軍によってすべて鎮圧されました。

5章
富国強兵
Wealth and Military Strength

【答え1】①イ　②ア　③ウ　【答え2】①イ　②ア　③ウ　【答え3】ウ
【答え4】army

50 The Lord of Army, Yamagata Aritomo and the Conscription Ordinance

陸軍卿（きょう）・山県有朋（やまがたありとも）と徴兵令

We will fight for our country!
お国のために戦うぞ！
徴兵令で、満20歳以上の成年男子に兵役の義務を課しました。
徴兵免役心得
免除規定
• 一家の主たる者
• 家のあとを継ぐ者
• 官立学校生徒
• 養子
All heads of household and students are exempted from military service...
一家の主や学生は兵役免除か…
徴兵令には、多くの免除規定がありました。
Even in the *Meiji* period, our living is still hard!
明治になっても、暮らしは大変なままじゃないか！
負担が増えた農民が血税一揆を起こしました。

51 The Settlement in Hokkaido and Farming Warriors

北海道開拓と屯田兵（とんでんへい）

① The *Meiji* government gave the *Ezo* region (蝦夷地) a new name and called it "*Hokkaido*" in 1869. ② Then the development comission (開拓使) was stationed (配置された) in order to develop agriculture (農業) and stock-farming (牧畜). ③ The *Sapporo* Agricultural College (札幌農学校) was established (設立された), and invited (招いた) Clark from the United States. ④ *Nitobe Inazo* and *Uchimura Kanzo* who studied here were greatly affected (大きな影響を受けた) by the spirit (精神) of Clark. ⑤ The government placed farming warriors (屯田兵) in *Hokkaido*. ⑥ The farming warriors did military training (軍事訓練) as well as (～をしながら) farming. ⑦ The two aims (ねらい) of this arrangement (配置) were to defend (守る) against Russia's Policy of Southward Expansion (南下政策) and allow (与える) warriors (士族) who lost their jobs and identities to make a living. ⑧ While the *Hokkaido* settlements were moving forward, the daily existence and culture of the Ainu natives gradually disappeared.

identities 身分 / make a living 生計を立てる / *Hokkaido* settlements 北海道開拓 / moving forward 進む / the daily existence 生活 / Ainu natives もともと住んでいたアイヌ人 / gradually しだいに / disappeared 消失した

和訳

①1869年、明治政府は蝦夷地(えぞち)に「北海道」という新しい名称をつけました。②そして農業や牧畜を発展させるため、開拓使を置きました。③札幌農学校をつくり、アメリカからクラークを招きました。④ここで学んだ新渡戸稲造(にとべいなぞう)や内村鑑三(うちむらかんぞう)は、クラークの精神に大きな影響を受けました。⑤政府は北海道に屯田兵を置きました。⑥屯田兵は、農業を営(いとな)みながら軍事訓練を行ないました。⑦屯田兵の設置には、ロシアの南下政策に対する防備と、仕事や身分を失った士族に生計(せいけい)を立てさせるという２つのねらいがありました。⑧北海道の開拓が進むいっぽう、昔からこの地に住んでいたアイヌの人々の生活や文化はしだいに失われていきました。

52 The Ryukyu Disposition and the Dispatching of Troops to Taiwan

琉球処分と台湾出兵（りゅうきゅう）

① During the *Edo* period (江戸時代), the Kingdom of *Ryukyu* (琉球王国) belonged to (〜に属した) the *Satsuma* Domain and paid tribute to (〜に朝貢した) Qing (清). ② In the *Meiji* period, Japan was opposed to (〜と対立していた) Qing regarding (〜について) the ascription (帰属) of *Ryukyu*. ③ In 1871, an incident (事件) took place (起こった) where shipwrecked people (漂流民) from *Ryukyu* were killed by Taiwanese local citizens (台湾の現地住民). ④ The *Meiji* government dispatched troops (出兵した) to Taiwan and the troops (軍隊) occupied (占領した) a part of Taiwan. ⑤ Through the British arbitration (調停), Qing had to pay compensation (賠償金) to Japan, and the Japanese troops withdrew (撤退した) from Taiwan. ⑥ At that time, it was recognized (認識された) in the international society (国際社会) that *Ryukyu* belonged to Japan. ⑦ In 1879, the

Meiji government decided to place *Okinawa* Prefecture
～を決めた　置く

there, instead of abolishing the Kingdom of *Ryukyu*.
～する代わりに　廃止する

⑧ This is called "the *Ryukyu* Disposition".
琉球処分

和訳

①江戸時代、琉球王国は薩摩藩に属しながら、清にも朝貢（ちょうこう）していました。②明治時代になり、琉球の帰属をめぐって日本は清と対立しました。③1871年、琉球の漂流民が台湾の現地住民に殺される事件が起こりました。④明治政府は台湾に出兵し、日本軍は台湾の一部を占領しました。⑤イギリスの調停により、清は日本に賠償金を払うことになり、日本軍は台湾から撤退しました。⑥この時、琉球は日本に帰属することが国際社会で認められました。⑦1879年、明治政府は琉球藩を廃止し、代わりに沖縄県を置くことを決定しました。⑧これを「琉球処分」といいます。

53 Demarcation
領土の画定

① It was agreed that the north of *Urup* Island in the
決められた　～の北　得撫島
Kurile Islands belonged to Russia, while the south of
千島列島　～に所属した
Etorofu Island was Japanese territory according to the
択捉島　日本の領土
Treaty of Peace and Amity between Japan and Russia
日露和親条約
at the end of the shogunate. ② *Karafuto* had become
幕末
the place where both Japanese and Russians resided.
居住した
③ The *Meiji* government sent *Enomoto Takeaki* to
Russia and he signed the Treaty of Saint Petersburg in
結んだ　樺太・千島交換条約
1875. ④ *Karafuto* became Russian territory and Japan
acquired Kurile Island under this treaty. ⑤ On the
得た　この条約により　これに対して
other hand, it was unclear where the *Ogasawara*
明らかでない
Islands belonged to. ⑥ The *Edo* shogunate declared
宣言した

the territorial rights over the Islands in the 1850s.
領有権 1850年代

⑦ The *Meiji* government announced to England and
宣言した

the United States that the *Ogasawara* Islands were Japanese territory in 1876. ⑧ As there were no objection from both countries, the *Ogasawara* Islands
異議

became territories of Japan.

和訳

①幕末期の日露和親条約により、千島(ちしま)列島の得撫島(うるっぷとう)以北はロシア領、択捉(えとろふ)島以南は日本領と定められていました。②樺太(からふと)は日本人とロシア人が共存する土地となっていました。③明治政府は、榎本武揚をロシアに派遣し、1875年、樺太・千島交換条約を結びました。④これにより、樺太はロシア領となり、日本は千島全島を手に入れました。⑤これに対して、小笠原(おがさわら)諸島は、所属が明確ではありませんでした。⑥江戸幕府は1850年代に領有を宣言しました。⑦1876年、明治政府も小笠原諸島は日本の領土であるとイギリス・アメリカに宣言しました。⑧両国から異議がなかったこともあり、小笠原諸島は日本領となりました。

54 The Ganghwa Island Incident and the Japan-Korea Treaty of Amity
江華島(こうかとう)事件と日朝修好条規

① A Japanese warship (軍艦), *Unyo*, was surveying (測量をしていた) an area of the ocean (海域) near the western coast (西岸) of Korea in 1875. ② When *Unyo* approached (接近した) Ganghwa Island (江華島) offshore (沖) of Seoul (ソウル), it was fired (砲撃された) by Korea. ③ *Unyo* fought back (反撃した) and destroyed (破壊した) the gun batteries (砲台) on Ganghwa Island. ④ Furthermore (さらに), it landed on (〜に上陸した) Yeongjong Island (永宗島) and occupied (占領した) it. ⑤ This is called "the Ganghwa Island Incident" (江華島事件). ⑥ It led to the opportunity (機会) for the *Meiji* government to pressure (圧力をかける) Korea, and they signed (結んだ) the Japan-Korea Treaty of Amity (日朝修好条規) the following year. ⑦ As a result (この結果), Korea which was under the Isolation Policy (鎖国) opened its country (開国した). ⑧ Japan forced (強制した) Korea to

accept extraterritoriality and tariff exemption in this
受け入れる 領事裁判権 関税の免除

treaty. ⑨ This was an unequal treaty which was
不平等条約

advantageous for Japan.
有利な

和訳

①1875年、朝鮮西岸の海域で日本の軍艦・雲揚(うんよう)号が測量を行なっていました。②雲揚号がソウル近郊の江華島に接近した時、朝鮮から砲撃を受けました。③雲揚号は応戦し、江華島の砲台を破壊しました。④さらに永宗島(えいそうとう)に上陸し、占領しました。⑤これを「江華島事件」といいます。⑥これを機に、明治政府は朝鮮に対し圧力をかけ、翌年日朝修好条規を結びました。⑦これにより、鎖国していた朝鮮は開国しました。⑧日朝修好条規では、朝鮮に対して領事裁判権を認めさせ、輸出入商品の関税を免除させました。⑨日本にとって有利な内容の不平等条約でした。

55 Land-Tax Reform

地租改正（ちそかいせい）

① During the *Edo* period, farmers paid rice as the tax.
農民 米 税

② Since the amount of rice production changed each
総計 米の生産量

year, the tax income was unstable. ③ The *Meiji*
税収 不安定な

government initiated a reform of the land and tax
着手した 改革 土地制度と税制

system. ④ The government allowed landowners and
認めた 地主

independent farmers to have land ownership. ⑤ The
自作農 土地所有権

government decided the land price and issued land
決めた 地価 発行した 地券

certificates to certify the landowners. ⑥ The
証明する

government announced the Land-Tax Reform
公布した 地租改正条例

Regulation in 1873. ⑦ It was decided that landowners

should pay tax by cash. ⑧ The tax rate was decided
税率

on 3% of the land price value. ⑨ A tax system was

organized and government finances became stable.
整えられた　政府の財政　安定した

⑩ However, this was still a heavy burden to the farmers, therefore a riot took place in various regions.
しかし　重い負担　そのために　一揆　各地

⑪ The government lowered the land-tax rate to 2.5% in 1877.
引き下げた　地租

和訳

①江戸時代、税は農民が米で納める方式でした。②米の生産量は毎年変わるので、税収は不安定でした。③明治政府は、土地制度と税制の改革に着手しました。④政府は、地主や自作農の土地所有権を認めました。⑤政府は、地価を定めて地券（ちけん）を発行し、土地所有者を明示しました。⑥1873年、政府は地租改正条例を公布しました。⑦税は、土地所有者が現金で納めることとなりました。⑧税率は地価の３％と定められました。⑨税制が整い、政府の財政は安定しました。⑩しかし、農民にとって重い負担は変わらなかったので、各地で一揆が起こりました。⑪1877年、政府は地租を2.5％に引き下げました。

56 The Gold Standard System and the National Bank Act

金本位制度と国立銀行条例

① The *Meiji* government started a reform of the
改革
monetary system. ② The government established the
貨幣制度 制定した
New Currency Regulations in 1871 and unified the
新貨条例 統一した
currency unit into *yen*, *sen* and *rin*. ③ The aim was to
貨幣単位 目的
introduce the gold standard system in which the
導入する 金本位制度
currency values were based on gold. ④ The gold
通貨の価値 ～に基礎を置いた
standard system was an international monetary system
国際的な通貨制度
at the end of 19th century. ⑤ There was a large quantity
～の終わり 19世紀 大量
of gold outflow abroad from Japan in the trade after
流出 海外に 貿易
opening the country. ⑥ Silver was used for payment
開国 ～に使われていた 決済
at ports. ⑦ The government established the National
開港地 国立銀行条例
Bank Act in 1872 in order to make bank bills
紙幣

exchangeable for gold. ⑧ Under the regulation, national
～と交換できる 条例

banks which could issue bank bills were established
発行する

across the country.
国の各地に

和訳

①明治政府は、貨幣制度の改革に着手しました。②1871年に新貨(しんか)条例を定め、貨幣の単位を円(えん)・銭(せん)・厘(りん)に統一しました。③通貨の価値の基準を金(きん)に置く金本位制度の導入を目指しました。④金本位制度は、19世紀末の国際的な通貨制度でした。⑤日本は開国後の貿易で、多くの金を海外に流出させていました。⑥開港地での決済には銀が使われていました。⑦政府は、金と交換できる紙幣をつくるため、1872年に国立銀行条例を定めました。⑧この条例にもとづき、紙幣の発行ができる国立銀行が各地につくられました。

57 The Tomioka Silk Factory and Government-run Factories

富岡(とみおか)製糸場と官営工場

① In the beginning of the *Meiji* period, trade in Japan was in deficit. ② In those days, the main exports of Japan was raw silk and tea. ③ The *Meiji* government tried to increase the production of raw silk and to reduce the trade deficit. ④ The government built a government-run yarn factory in *Tomioka* of *Gunma* Prefecture. ⑤ *Tomioka* was basically famous for silk cultivation. ⑥ The new machines were imported to *Tomioka* Silk Factory from France and it started its operation in 1872. ⑦ There were a great number of young women working at the factory and most were daughters of warriors. ⑧ Other than the *Tomioka* Silk

In the beginning of: ～の初期
was in deficit: 赤字だった
In those days: 当時
exports: 輸出品
raw silk: 生糸
tried to: ～しようとした
increase: 増やす
the production: 生産
reduce: 減少させる
the trade deficit: 貿易赤字
a government-run yarn factory: 官営の製糸工場
Gunma Prefecture: 群馬県
basically: もともと
famous for: ～で有名な
silk cultivation: 養蚕
were imported: 輸入された
Tomioka Silk Factory: 富岡製糸場
operation: 操業
a great number of: たくさんの
warriors: 士族
Other than: ～以外に

Factory, the government also built many government-run factories. ⑨ A cement factory (セメント工場) built in *Fukagawa* of *Tokyo* and a clothing factory (服飾工場) built in *Senju* are famous (有名な).

和訳

①明治時代の初期、日本の貿易は赤字でした。②当時の日本の主な輸出品は、生糸(きいと)や茶でした。③明治政府は、生糸の生産を増やし、貿易赤字を減らそうとしました。④政府は、群馬県の富岡に官営の製糸工場をつくりました。⑤富岡は、もともと養蚕(ようさん)のさかんな土地でした。⑥富岡製糸場にはフランスから新しい機械が輸入され、1872年に操業を開始しました。⑦富岡製糸場で働いていたのは若い女性が多く、ほとんどが士族の娘でした。⑧富岡製糸場のほかにも、政府は多くの官営工場をつくりました。⑨東京の深川(ふかがわ)につくられたセメント工場や、千住(せんじゅ)につくられた服飾(ふくしょく)工場などが有名です。

58

Shibusawa Eiichi and the Encouragement of New Industry

渋沢栄一（しぶさわえいいち）と殖産興業

① *Shibusawa Eiichi* was born to a wealthy farm family
～の家に生まれた　裕福な　農家

in *Saitama* Prefecture in 1840, and served *Tokugawa*
仕えた

Yoshinobu. ② *Shibusawa Eiichi* participated in an
～に参加した

International Exhibition held in Paris and watched the
万国博覧会　～で開かれた

advanced technology of Europe through his own eyes.
進んだ　技術

③ After returning home, he became a public official
役人

of the *Meiji* government. ④ The *Meiji* government

tried to create various kinds of modern industries in
～しようとした　さまざまな　種類　近代産業

the nation in order to build up sufficient economic
増強する　十分な　経済力

strength. ⑤ This is called "the Encouragement of New
殖産興業

Industry". ⑥ After *Shibusawa* left the government, he
去った

was involved in the establishment of a wide variety of
～に携わった　設立　さまざまな

companies, starting with a bank, then a gas company,
～をはじめ

an insurance company, a paper-manufacturing company,
保険会社 製紙会社

a railroad company, as well as the stock market.
鉄道会社 証券取引所

⑦ *Shibusawa* is called "the Father of Modern Industry in Japan".
日本近代産業の父

和訳

①渋沢栄一は、1840年、埼玉県の豊かな農家に生まれ、徳川慶喜に仕（つか）えました。②渋沢栄一はパリで行なわれた万国博覧会（ばんこくはくらんかい）に出向き、ヨーロッパの進んだ技術を目の当たりにしました。③帰国後、明治政府の役人となりました。④明治政府は、豊かな経済力をつけるために、さまざまな近代産業を国内に興（おこ）そうとしました。⑤これを「殖産興業」といいます。⑥渋沢は政府を去ったのち、銀行をはじめ、ガス会社、保険会社、製紙会社、鉄道会社、証券取引所などさまざまな企業の設立に携（たずさ）わりました。⑦渋沢は、「日本近代産業の父」といわれています。

59

From Wealthy Merchants to Industrial Conglomerates

豪商から財閥へ

① The financially-stricken *Meiji* government expected
経済的に苦しい　期待した

the economic power of *Mitsui*, *Mitsubishi*, *Sumitomo*
経済力

and *Yasuda*, which were called wealthy merchants.
豪商

② *Mitsui* became wealthy from running an exchange
裕福な　両替商

store and a Japanese *Kimono* shop in the *Edo* period.
呉服店　江戸時代

③ It had become stronger by establishing the first
設立　第一国立銀行

national bank and *Mitsui* & Co., Ltd. after the *Meiji*
三井物産

period started. ④ *Mitsubishi* was established at the end

of the shogunate and expanded its business to a shipping
勢力を伸ばした　海運業

industry. ⑤ *Sumitomo* succeeded in doing refining
成功した　精錬業

business of copper in the *Edo* period. ⑥ It continued to
銅

develop its business mainly in the *Besshi* Copper Mine
事業を発展させる　別子銅山

in *Ehime* Prefecture even in the *Meiji* period. ⑦ *Yasuda* built up a fortune (巨大な富(財産)を築いた) by doing exchange business at the end of the shogunate and it expanded centering on (～を中心に発展した) financial business (金融業). ⑧ These wealthy merchants formed groups (グループをつくった) called "Industrial Conglomerates" (財閥) and became the center of (～の中心に) Japanese Industry, respectively (それぞれ).

和訳

①財政が苦しかった明治政府は、豪商と呼ばれた三井(みつい)・三菱(みつびし)・住友(すみとも)・安田(やすだ)ら大商人の経済力に期待しました。②三井は江戸時代、両替商や呉服店などで財を成しました。③明治時代に入ってからは第一国立銀行や三井物産などをつくり、勢力を伸ばしました。④三菱は幕末に設立され、海運業に進出しました。⑤住友は江戸時代に銅の精錬(せいれん)で成功を収めました。⑥明治時代に入ってからも、愛媛県の別子(べっし)銅山を中心に事業を発展させました。⑦安田は、幕末に両替商で巨大な富を築き、金融業中心に成長しました。⑧これらの豪商はそれぞれ「財閥」と呼ばれるグループをつくり、日本の産業の中心となっていきました。

60 The Establishment of the Bank of Japan and the Matsukata Finance Administration

日本銀行設立と松方（まつかた）財政

① The *Meiji* government spent a large amount of
出費がかさんだ
money doing several reforms. ② It also spent a lot of
諸改革
money on military expenses during the *Seinan* War.
軍事費
③ The government and the national bank issued a lot
国立銀行　発行した
of paper bills to cover the spending. ④ As a result,
紙幣　出費をおぎなう　その結果
inflation occurred and prices were raised.
起こった　物価　上昇した
⑤ *Matsukata Masayoshi* took the position of lord of
就任した　大蔵卿
treasury in 1881. ⑥ *Matsukata* adopted the Fiscal
採用した　緊縮財政
Austerity Policy to cut down on annual expenditures
削減　歳出の
and increase tax. ⑦ He established the Bank of Japan
増税　日本銀行
in 1882 and decided that only the Bank of Japan could
issue paper bills. ⑧ In 1885, he issued convertible
兌換紙幣

currency allowing the exchange between paper bills and
交換

silver. ⑨ With *Matsukata's* policy, inflation came to
銀貨 おさまった

an end. ⑩ However, it suddenly turned to recession.
不況

⑪ In farming villages, the price of rice and raw silk

declined, and the farmers' day to day life became
下落した 日々の暮らし 厳しくなった

severe.

和訳

①明治政府は、諸改革を行なったため出費がかさみました。②西南戦争でも、多額の軍事費を支出しました。③これらの出費をおぎなうため、政府や国立銀行は紙幣を大量に発行しました。④その結果、インフレーションが起こり、物価は上昇しました。⑤1881年、松方正義(まさよし)が大蔵卿に就任しました。⑥松方は、歳出の削減、増税などの徹底的な緊縮財政を採りました。⑦1882年には日本銀行を設立し、日本銀行だけが紙幣を発行できることにしました。⑧1885年、銀貨と交換ができる兌換(だかん)紙幣を発行させました。⑨松方の政策により、インフレーションはおさまりました。⑩しかし、一転して不況となりました。⑪農村では米や生糸の価格が下落し、農民の暮らしは厳しくなりました。

おさらいクイズ

【問題1】次の英語が表わす日本語を、あとのア～ウから選びなさい。

① the land price
② the Japan-Korea Treaty of Amity
③ government-run factories

ア 官営工場　　イ 地価　　ウ 日朝修好条約

【問題2】次の日本語が表わす英語を、あとのア～ウから選びなさい。

① 屯田兵
② 生糸
③ 地券

ア land certificate
イ raw silk
ウ farming warriors

【問題3】次の英文の意味を、あとのア～ウから選びなさい。

The government and the national bank issued a lot of paper bills to cover the spending.

ア 政府や国立銀行は、これらの出費をおぎなうため、紙幣を大量に発行しました。
イ 政府や国立銀行は、これらの出費を増やすため、紙幣を大量に発行しました。
ウ 政府や民間銀行は、これらの出費をおぎなうため、紙幣を大量に発行しました。

【問題4】次の英文を訳しなさい。

The *Meiji* government started a reform of the monetary system.

6章
文明開化
Cultural Enlightenment

【答え1】①イ　②ウ　③ア　【答え2】①ウ　②イ　③ア　【答え3】ア

【答え4】明治政府は、貨幣制度の改革に着手しました。

61

Cultural Enlightenment
文明開化

明治政府は、西洋の技術や制度だけでなく、衣・食・住などの文化や生活習慣もさかんに取り入れました。通りには、レンガ造りの２階建て洋館が建ち並びました。人力車や乗合馬車などの新しい乗りものが登場しました。

Hats and parasols are symbols of cultural enlightenment.
帽子やパラソルは文明開化の象徴だ。
Wow, it lit up!
あっ、ついた！
夕方になると、ガス灯に灯がともりました。
洋服を着て、帽子をかぶり、靴をはく人たちが現われました。
By tapping on the cropped head, you will hear the sound of cultural enlightenment.
ザンギリ頭をたたいてみれば、文明開化の音がする。
まげを切って、ザンギリ頭にする人が増えました。
Beef tastes delicious.
牛肉はうまいなぁ。
牛肉を日本風に煮て食べる「牛鍋」が流行しました。

62

The Opening of the Railroad

鉄道開通

① The Japanese actually saw steam locomotives run
実際に　蒸気機関車

for the first time, when the American envoy Perry
はじめて　使節

arrived for the second time. ② This steam locomotive
再び来航した

was a model which was one of the tributes given by the
模型　献上品

president of the United States to the shogunate. ③ The
アメリカ大統領

Meiji government worked on the construction of
～に取り組んだ　建設

railroads as one of the Encouragement of New Industry,
鉄道　～のひとつとして　殖産興業

which was essential for the development of the modern
欠かせない　発展　近代産業

industry. ④ The construction was recommended by
建設　勧められた（推薦された）

Parks, an English minister, and England raised funds
公使　調達した　資金

and dispatched technicians. ⑤ The government railroad
派遣した　技術者　官営鉄道

started between *Shinbashi* and *Yokohama* for the first
開通した

time in 1872. ⑥ Afterward, railroads between *Osaka*
その後
and *Kobe*, *Kyoto* and *Osaka* were also opened. ⑦ These railroads connected the trading ports and big cities,
結びつけた 貿易港
which greatly contributed to the development of industry.
貢献した

和訳

①日本人が実際に走る蒸気機関車をはじめて見たのは、アメリカ使節・ペリーが再び来航した時です。②この蒸気機関車は模型で、アメリカ大統領から幕府へ贈られた献上品の1つでした。③明治政府は殖産興業の一環として、近代産業の発展に欠かせない鉄道の建設に取り組みました。④建設はイギリス公使・パークスの勧めによるもので、イギリスが資金調達と技術者の派遣を行ないました。⑤1872年、新橋～横浜間に、はじめて官営の鉄道が開通しました。⑥その後、大阪～神戸間、京都～大阪間も開通しました。⑦これらの鉄道は貿易港と大都市を結びつけ、産業の発展に大きく貢献しました。

63 The Opening of the Telephone Network and Postal System

電話開通と郵便制度

① The Telegraph System which was the predecessor
電信 前身
of telephones was opened between *Tokyo* and
電話
Yokohama for the first time in 1869 and it had almost
ほぼ
spread nationwide in the 1880s. ② The Telephone
全国に普及した 電話交換
Exchange System started between *Tokyo* and *Yokohama*
in 1890. ③ In those days, people called operators by
当時 交換手
turning the crank on the telephone and giving the
ハンドル
receiver's number to connect. ④ The Postal System
接続する 郵便制度
started to replace the express messenger of the *Edo*
～に代わる 飛脚
period in 1871. ⑤ Mail boxes were placed everywhere
ポスト
in towns and on streets, and the national postal network
全国郵便網
where the use of stamps with a flat rate was settled.
切手 均一料金 整備された

⑥ In the beginning, mail boxes were wooden (木製の) and square-shaped (四角の) but later on (のちに), iron (鉄製の) boxes which were fire proof (火事に強い) were invented (考案された).

和訳

①電話の前身である電信は、1869年に東京〜横浜間ではじめて開通し、1880年代にはほぼ全国に普及しました。②1890年には、東京〜横浜間で電話交換が開始されました。③当時の電話は、電話機についているハンドルを回して電話局の交換手を呼び出し、相手の番号を告げて接続してもらうというシステムでした。④郵便制度は、江戸時代の飛脚(ひきゃく)に代わるものとして、1871年に開始されました。⑤町や街道に郵便ポストが置かれ、切手の使用により均一料金で利用できる全国郵便網(もう)が整備されました。⑥当初のポストは木製の四角い箱でしたが、のちに火事に強い鉄製のものが考案されました。

64 The Use of the Solar Calendar
太陽暦の採用

① Until the *Edo* period, the lunar calendar had been used in Japan. ② When the *Meiji* period started, Japan began to negotiate with western countries which used the solar calendar, and found that it caused some inconvenience. ③ The *Meiji* government abolished the lunar calendar that was used before and decided to use the solar calendar. ④ The lunar calendar is a calendar designed based on the phases of the moon. ⑤ In the lunar calendar, there were roughly 354 days in a year, therefore, a year with 13 months in a leap year was established once every three years. ⑥ In contrast, the solar calendar put basis on the cycle of the earth going round the sun, and it is still

Until：〜まで　the lunar calendar：太陰暦　negotiate：交渉する　the solar calendar：太陽暦　found：見つかった　inconvenience：不都合　abolished：廃止した　designed：つくられた　based on：〜をもとにして　the phases of the moon：月の満ち欠け　roughly：およそ　therefore：そのために　a leap year：うるう年　once every three years：3年に1回　In contrast：これに対し　the cycle：周期

being used up to the present time. ⑦ The government
現在

decided that December 3, 1872 (*Meiji* 5) was January 1st in the following year due to the adoption of the
～のため 採用

solar calendar. ⑧ Therefore, the year of *Meiji* 5 ended on December 2nd, which only had about 11 months.

和訳

①江戸時代まで、日本国内では太陰暦(たいいん)が使われていました。②明治時代に入り、太陽暦を使う欧米諸国と交渉するようになると、不都合が生じるようになりました。③明治政府は、それまでの太陰暦を廃止して、太陽暦を採用することにしました。④太陰歴は、月の満ち欠けをもとにしてつくられた暦(こよみ)です。⑤太陰暦では、1年がおよそ354日になるため、1年を13カ月とするうるう年をほぼ3年に1回設けていました。⑥これに対し、太陽暦は、地球が太陽を回る周期を基準としたもので、現在も使われている暦です。⑦政府は、太陽暦の採用にともない、明治5年(1872年)の12月3日を翌年の1月1日としました。⑧このため、明治5年は12月2日までとなり、ほぼ11カ月しかありませんでした。

65 The School System and Compulsory Education

学制(がくせい)と義務教育

① The *Meiji* government thought that the spread of education (教育の普及) was required (必要とした) in order to develop the country to catch up with (～に追いつく) western countries. ② The school system (学制) was issued (発布された) in 1872. ③ All boys and girls, 6 years and over (6歳以上の) were to receive elementary school (小学校) education under this system. ④ Elementary schools were established across the country (全国に) either by using small cram schools (寺子屋) and temples (寺院) or new school houses were built. ⑤ However, there were riots (一揆) against the school system in various regions (各地で) because school fees (学費) were too expensive (高価すぎる) and there were no workers at home if the children went to school. ⑥ In the following year of the issuance of the school system, there were only 40% of boys and 15% of girls who were actually attending elementary schools.

実際に出席していた

和訳

①明治政府は、国家を発展させて欧米諸国に追いつくためには、教育の普及が必要だと考えました。②1872年、学制を公布しました。③これにより、6歳以上のすべての男女は、小学校教育を受けることになりました。④校舎は寺子屋(てらこや)や寺院などを利用したり、新しく建設したりして、全国各地に小学校がつくられました。⑤しかし、授業料が高すぎる、子どもが学校へ行くと家の働き手がなくなるなどの理由から、学制に反対する一揆が各地で起きました。⑥学制発布の翌年、実際に小学校に通った子どもたちは、男子は40%ほど、女子は15%あまりしかいませんでした。

66 The Imperial University Ordinance and Private Schools

帝国大学令と私立学校

① The Imperial University Ordinance was announced
帝国大学令 公布された

in 1886 in order to educate people who played a central
～するために 教育する 中枢を担う

role in the nation. ② Based on this, *Tokyo* University
これにもとづいて 東京大学

was categorized as an Imperial Universities by
改組された 帝国大学

combining with the Imperial College of Engineering.
～と組み合わせる 工部大学校

③ Seven imperial universities named after districts or
地区

regions such as *Kyoto*, *Tohoku* and *Kyushu* were
地方

established. ④ During the same time, apart from
設立された いっぽう ～は別として

universities managed by the government, private
管理された 政府 私立学校

schools with their own education were established.
独自の教育

⑤ *Keio Gijyuku* (now *Keio Gijyuku* University) by
現・慶應義塾大学

Fukuzawa Yukichi, *Tokyo* Vocational College (now
東京専門学校

Waseda University) by *Okuma Shigenobu*, and *Doshisha* (now *Doshisha* University) by *Niijima Jo* are famous（有名な）. ⑥ These private schools developed（育んだ） a school tradition（校風） that was free and active, and sent out（送り出した） outstanding（優秀な） people into the political community（政界） and the business world（経済界）.

和訳

①国家の中枢（ちゅうすう）を担（にな）う人材の育成を目的として、1886年に帝国大学令が公布されました。②これにもとづき、東京大学が工部大学校と合わせて帝国大学に改組されました。③京都、東北、九州など、地名や地方名を冠（かん）した７つの帝国大学が設立されました。④いっぽう、政府が管理する大学とは別に、独自の教育を行なう私立学校が創設されました。⑤福沢諭吉（ふくざわゆきち）の慶應義塾（けいおうぎじゅく）（現・慶應義塾大学）、大隈重信（おおくましげのぶ）の東京専門学校（現・早稲田大学）、新島襄（にいじまじょう）の同志社（どうししゃ）（現・同志社大学）などが有名です。⑥これらの私立学校では、自由活発な学風が育（はぐく）まれ、優秀な人材を政界や経済界などに送り込みました。

67 The Establishment of Tokyo Art School

東京美術学校設立

① Due to cultural enlightenment, there was a trend
文明開化 風潮
that anything that came from western culture was
superior in any field. ② Traditional Japanese culture
すぐれている どんな分野でも 日本の伝統文化
was considered as "out of date" and it appeared that a
みなされた 古くさい
lot of Japanese threw away Japanese paintings, Japanese
捨てた 日本画 浮世絵
woodblock prints and Buddha statues or sold them at
仏像 売った
low prices. ③ Fenollosa, who was invited from
安価で 招かれた
America as a lecturer at *Tokyo* University, was
講師
impressed with the greatness of traditional Japanese
～に感動した すばらしさ
Arts and he thought that they should be valued.
大切にするべき
④ Fenollosa and his student, *Okakura Tenshin* at the
university, devoted themselves to the reconstruction
～に身をささげた 復興

of Japanese Arts by investigating local fine arts and
調査 各地の美術品

carrying on the study of it. ⑤ *Okakura Tenshin*
続けること 研究

established the *Tokyo* Art School (now the *Tokyo*
設立した 東京美術学校 現・東京芸術大学

National University of Fine Arts & Music) with

Fenollosa in 1887. ⑥ Many outstanding Japanese
優秀な

painters graduated from this school.
卒業した

和訳

①文明開化により、どのような分野でも西洋のものがすぐれているという風潮が生まれました。②日本の伝統文化は「古いもの」とみなされ、日本画や浮世絵、仏像などを捨てたり、安い値段で売ったりする日本人がたくさん現われました。③東京大学の講師としてアメリカから招かれたフェノロサは、日本の伝統美術のすばらしさに感動し、その良さを大切にしなければならないと考えました。④フェノロサは、大学の教え子である岡倉天心(おかくらてんしん)とともに、各地の美術品を調査し、日本美術の研究を進め、その復興に努めました。⑤岡倉天心は、フェノロサとともに1887年に東京美術学校(現・東京芸術大学)を設立しました。⑥この学校から、多くのすぐれた日本人画家が生まれました。

68 'Gakumon no Susume' and 'Ukigumo'

『学問のすゝめ』と『浮雲』

①Due to Cultural Enlightenment, Western individualism (個人主義) and liberalism (自由主義) started to be introduced (紹介された), and were widely accepted (広く受け入れられた). ② *Fukuzawa Yukichi* aimed (目指した) at changing the Japanese feudalistic idea (封建的な考えかた) and wrote '*Gakumon no susume*'. ③ Its starting phrase (書き出しの言葉), "Heaven doesn't make a man better than others, nor does it make a man worse than others" (「天は人の上に人をつくらず、人の下に人をつくらず」) is well known. ④ He insisted (説いた) that man should be equal (平等な) regardless of (〜に関係なく) his social status (地位), and man should study and become independent (独立する) and rise in the world (身を立てる) by studying in order to develop the country. ⑤ *Futabatei Shimei* wrote a novel (小説) called '*Ukigumo*' using colloquialism (口語体) which is the unification (言文一致)

of the written and spoken forms of a language. ⑥ In those days, the literacy style (文語体) based on Japanese poems (和歌) and Japanese classics (古典) was commonly (一般に) used, therefore, '*Ukigumo*' brought huge impact on (～に大きな影響を与えた) modern literature (近代文学).

和訳

①文明開化によって、西洋の個人主義や自由主義などが紹介されるようになり、広く受け入れられました。②福沢諭吉は、日本の古い封建的な考えかたを変えることを目指して、『学問のすゝめ』を書きました。③「天は人の上に人をつくらず、人の下に人をつくらず」という書き出しで知られています。④人は身分に関係なく誰もが平等であることや、国を発展させるためには学問を学んで個人が独立し、身を立てることが大切であると説きました。⑤二葉亭四迷(ふたばていしめい)は、言文一致(げんぶんいっち)という話し言葉の文章で、『浮雲』という小説を書きました。⑥当時は、和歌や古典にもとづく文語体(ぶんごたい)の文章が中心であったため、『浮雲』は近代文学に大きな影響を与えました。

69 Hired Foreign Advisors

お雇い外国人

オランダの法学者・フルベッキは、岩倉使節団の派遣を進言し、「近代建設の父」といわれています。

クラークは、札幌農学校の初代教頭を務めました。

モースは、大森貝塚を発見しました。

コンドルは、建築学を教え、鹿鳴館、ニコライ堂などを設計・建築しました。

ヘボンは、日本初の和英・英和辞典を完成させました。

ベルツは、大学で医学を教えながら、寄生虫病の研究を行ないました。

70 The New Noble System and the Social Interaction Hall called Rokumeikan
華族制度と鹿鳴館（ろくめいかん）

① The Noble Family Ordinance (華族令) was issued (発令された) in 1884 and in addition to (〜に加えて) former court nobles (旧公家) and former feudal lords (旧大名), people who dedicated to (〜に功労のあった) the nation were presented a noble title (爵位) after the *Meiji* Restoration (明治維新). ② As a result, many of the high-ranking government officials (政府高官) newly became noblemen (華族). ③ Noblemen enjoyed ball parties (舞踏会) with foreign diplomats (外国人外交官) almost every night at *Rokumeikan* built in *Hibiya*, *Tokyo*. ④ *Rokumeikan* was a luxurious (豪華な) Renaissance-style (ルネサンス様式の) building built as a place for social interaction (社交) to promote (促進する) the negotiation (交渉) of the treaty revision (条約改正). ⑤ Noblemen attended (出席した) the parties accompanying (〜をともなって) wives

and daughters wearing evening dresses. ⑥ Although
イブニング・ドレス / けれども

there was no remarkable diplomatic accomplishment,
めざましい / 外交的な成果

it was a good opportunity for Japanese of upper social
機会 / 上流階級

class to learn social interaction in a western manner.
西洋式の

和訳

①1884年、華族令が出され、これまでの旧公家・旧大名らに加えて、明治維新以降、国家に功労のあった人々にも爵位(しゃくい)が与えられました。②この結果、政府高官の多くが華族となりました。③華族たちは、東京の日比谷(ひびや)に建てられた鹿鳴館で、毎晩のように外国人外交官と舞踏会(ぶとうかい)を楽しみました。④鹿鳴館は、条約改正交渉を促進するため、社交の場として建設された豪華なルネサンス様式の建物でした。⑤彼らは、イブニング・ドレスを身にまとった夫人や令嬢をともなって舞踏会に出席しました。⑥めざましい外交的な成果をおさめることはできませんでしたが、上流階級の日本人が西洋式の社交を学ぶ良い機会となりました。

おさらいクイズ

【問題1】次の英語が表わす日本語を、あとのア～ウから選びなさい。

① express messenger
② lunar calendar
③ Imperial University

ア 帝国大学　　イ 太陰暦　　ウ 飛脚

【問題2】次の日本語が表わす英語を、あとのア～ウから選びなさい。

① 学制
② 太陽暦
③ 文明開化

ア cultural enlightenment
イ school system
ウ solar calendar

【問題3】次の英文の意味を、あとのア～ウから選びなさい。

Traditional Japanese culture was considered out of date.

ア 日本の伝統文化は、古いものから外されました。
イ 日本の伝統文化は、古いものとみなされました。
ウ 日本の伝統文化は、古いものとして見直されました。

【問題4】次の英文の(　)にあてはまる1語を書きなさい。

The railroads connected the trading ports and big cities, which greatly (　　) to the development of industry.
鉄道は貿易港と大都市を結びつけ、産業の発達に大きく貢献しました。

7章
自由民権運動
The Freedom and People's Rights Movement

【答え1】①ウ ②イ ③ア 【答え2】①イ ②ウ ③ア 【答え3】イ
【答え4】contributed

71 The Government of Domain Groups
藩閥政治

① The main positions of the *Meiji* government and the military were occupied by the people of the *Satsuma*, *Choshu*, *Tosa*, and *Saga* Domains. ② Especially, the politicians who came from the *Satsuma* and *Choshu* Domains dominated the power exclusively. ③ This system of government administration is called "the Government of Domain Groups". ④ The main leaders of the government were *Kuroda Kiyotaka* (*Satsuma*), *Matsukata Masayoshi* (*Satsuma*), *Ito Hirobumi* (*Choshu*), *Yamagata Aritomo* (*Choshu*), *Katsura Taro* (*Choshu*), and *Okuma Shigenobu* (*Saga*) along with others. ⑤ They all took office as the prime minister.

main positions: 要職
military: 軍
were occupied by: ～によって占められていた
the politicians: 政治家
dominated: 支配した
the power: 権力
exclusively: 独占的に
system of government administration: 政治形態
the Government of Domain Groups: 藩閥政治
The main leaders: 主な指導者
took office as: ～に就任した
the prime minister: 首相

⑥ The Government of Domain Groups contradicted 相反した parliamentary politics. 議会政治 ⑦ After a while, やがて the Freedom and People's Rights Movement, 自由民権運動 that criticized 批判した this system of government administration and demanded ～を要求した for the Establishment 設立 of a Representative Assembly, 民撰議院 became active. さかんになった

和訳

①明治政府と軍の要職は、薩摩藩・長州藩・土佐藩・佐賀藩の出身者によって占められていました。②なかでも薩摩・長州藩出身の政治家が権力を独占していました。③この政治形態を「藩閥政治」といいます。④藩閥の主（おも）な指導者は黒田清隆（くろだきよたか）（薩摩）、松方正義（薩摩）、伊藤博文（長州）、山県有朋（長州）、桂太郎（かつらたろう）（長州）、大隈重信（佐賀）らでした。⑤彼らはいずれも首相に就任しています。⑥藩閥政治は議会政治と相反（あいはん）するものでした。⑦やがて、この政治形態を批判し、民撰議院（みんせんぎいん）設立を要求する自由民権運動がさかんになりました。

72

The Coup of Meiji 14
明治十四年の政変

① The Abolition of the development commission
廃止 開拓使

was decided in 1881. ② The head of the commission,
決められた 長官

Kuroda Kiyotaka tried to sell governmental facilities
〜しようとした 官有の 施設

and equipments at low prices to merchants. ③ When
設備 安価で 商人

it came to light, *Okuma Shigenobu* severely criticized
このことが明るみに出て 厳しく批判した

Kuroda Kiyotaka. ④ At that time, *Okuma Shigenobu*

insisted on the Establishment of Constitution based on
〜を主張した 憲法の制定 〜にもとづいた

a Parliamentary Cabinet System with reference to the
議院内閣制 〜を参考にした

British system and the early opening of the National
早期の開設 国会

Diet. ⑤ While, *Iwakura Tomomi* and *Ito Hirobumi*

opposed against *Okuma Shigenobu*, and urged that it
〜に反対した 主張した

should take time to establish a constitution with strong
時間をかける 君主権の強い

monarchical power like Germany. ⑥ *Ito Hirobumi* brought *Okuma Shigenobu* down and cancelled the disposal sale of governmental properties of the Development Commission. ⑦ This is called "the Coup of *Meiji* 14".

～を失脚させた　中止した　払い下げ　官有物　明治十四年の政変

和訳

①1881年、開拓使の廃止が決まりました。②開拓使の長官・黒田清隆は、官有の施設や設備を商人に安値で払い下げようとしました。③この行為が明るみに出て、大隈重信は黒田清隆を厳しく批判しました。④当時、大隈重信は、イギリスを参考にした議院内閣制にもとづく憲法の制定と早期の国会開設を主張していました。⑤いっぽう、岩倉具視や伊藤博文は、時間をかけてドイツのように君主権の強い憲法を制定することを唱え、大隈重信と対立していました。⑥伊藤博文は、大隈重信を失職させ、開拓使官有物の払い下げを中止しました。⑦これを「明治十四年の政変」といいます。

73

A Petition for the Establishment of a Representative Assembly

民撰(みんせん)議(ぎ)院(いん)設立建白書

① *Itagaki Taisuke*, *Goto Shojiro*, *Eto Shinpei*, *Soejima Taneomi*, *Yuri Kosei*, and *Okamoto Kenzaburo* submitted (提出した) a Petition for the Establishment of a Representative Assembly (民撰議院設立建白書), to the government in January of 1874. ② They were defeated (敗れた) by the political strife (政争) over the Policy of Conquering Korea (征韓論), and after they left (離れた) the government, they had been carrying out (実行していた) anti-government activities (反政府運動). ③ This petition (建白書(嘆願書)) was to demand the government to establish the National Diet. ④ *Itagaki* and others formed a Diet-establishing Union (国会期成同盟) in order to promote (展開する) a wider movement of opening the National Diet in 1880. ⑤ The union submitted a petition to the government to open the National Diet.

⑥ However, the government rejected this petition.
却下した

⑦ People in the union were dissatisfied with the
不満を抱いた

government's response. ⑧ Therefore, the movement of
対応

opening the National Diet became even more fired up.
さらに盛り上がるようになった

和訳

①1874年１月、板垣退助、後藤象二郎、江藤新平、副島種臣、由利公正、岡本健三郎らは、政府に対し、民撰議院設立の建白書を提出しました。②彼らは征韓論の政争に敗れ、政府を離れて以降、反政府運動を行なっていたのです。③建白書は、政府に国会の開設を求めるものでした。④板垣らは、国会開設の運動を広く展開するため、1880年、国会期成同盟を結成しました。⑤国会期成同盟は政府に対し、国会開設の請願書を提出しました。⑥ところが、政府はこの請願を却下しました。⑦国会期成同盟の人々は、政府の対応に強い不満を抱きました。⑧そして国会開設の運動は、さらに盛り上がることになりました。

74 The Imperial Edict for Opening the National Diet

国会開設の詔（みことのり）

① The Freedom and People's Rights Movement
自由民権運動
demanding the opening the National Diet fired up
国会開設　盛り上がっていた
even more. ② The government issued the assembly
集会条例
regulations and cracked down on radical movements.
～を取り締まった　急進的な　運動
③ However, the growing demand of opening the National Diet came from within the government.
～の中で
④ At that time, the incident of the disposal sale of
事件　払い下げ
government properties of the development commission
官有物　開拓使
took place, and criticism toward the government
起こった　～に対する批判
kept growing. ⑤ Moreover, by *Okuma Shigenobu*
さらに
criticizing this incident within the government and
批判した
getting expelled (the Coup of *Meiji* 14), it triggered
追放された　明治十四年の政変　引きおこした

violent public opinions. ⑥ In order to calm this uproar,
激しい 世論 しずめる 騒動

the government announced "the Imperial Edict for Opening the National Diet" in 1881. ⑦ "The Imperial Edict" means the Emperor's will. ⑧ By this edict, the government promised to open the Diet in 1890, nine years later.

発表した 国会開設の詔 詔(勅諭) 意思 勅諭 ～を約束した

和訳

①国会開設を要求する自由民権運動は、盛り上がりを見せていました。②政府は集会条例を制定して、急進的な運動を取り締まりました。③しかし、政府内からも国会開設の声が上がっていました。④この頃、開拓使官有物払い下げ事件が起こり、政府への批判は高まっていました。⑤さらに、この事件を政府内から批判していた大隈重信が追放されたこと(明治十四年の政変)で、世論は激化しました。⑥これをしずめるため、政府は1881年、「国会開設の詔」を出しました。⑦「詔(勅諭〈ちょくゆ〉)」とは、天皇の意思表示のことです。⑧この詔により、9年後の1890年に国会を開設することを国民に約束しました。

75 A Constitution Created by Private Citizens
私擬憲法

① In 1881, the Liberal Party (自由党) led by (〜を党首とする) *Itagaki Taisuke* was formed right after the Imperial Edict for Opening the National Diet (国会開設の詔) was announced (発表された). ② The parent organization (母体組織) of the Liberal Party was the Diet-establishing Union (国会期成同盟). ③ The Constitutional Reform Party (立憲改進党) led by *Okuma Shigenobu* was formed in 1882. ④ The Liberal Party mainly consisted of (〜から成る) warriors (士族) and small landlords (小地主), and they were radicals (急進派). ⑤ The Constitutional Reform Party was mainly organized (組織された) by wealthy merchants (大商人) and big landlords (大地主), and they were moderates (穏健派). ⑥ Private citizens (一般市民) such as individuals (個人) or common people (民衆) who made a draft of the constitution (憲法案) appeared (現われた).

⑦ This Constitution Draft is called "a Constitution created by private citizens" (私擬憲法). ⑧ "The draft of the Japanese Constituition" (日本国国憲案) by *Ueki Emori*, "the draft of a Constitution created by private citizens" (私擬憲法案) by *Kojunsha* and "the Itsukaichi Constitution draft" (五日市憲法草案) prepared (立案された) by the people living in *Itsukaichi* (now *Akiruno* City, *Tokyo*) are well known.

和訳

①1881年、国会開設の詔が出された直後、板垣退助を党首とする自由党(じゆうとう)が結成されました。②自由党は国会期成同盟を母体にしていました。③1882年には、大隈重信を党首とする立憲改進党(りっけんかいしん)が結成されました。④自由党は、士族や小地主が中心で急進的でした。⑤立憲改進党は、大商人や大地主で組織され、穏健派(おんけん)でした。⑥憲法案をつくる個人や民衆も現われました。⑦こうした憲法案を「私擬憲法」といいます。⑧植木枝盛(うえきえもり)の「日本国国憲案」や、交詢社(こうじゅんしゃ)による「私擬憲法案」、五日市(いつかいち)(現・東京都あきる野市)の人々がつくった「五日市憲法草案」などが知られています。

76

Even if Itagaki Dies...

板垣死すとも…

板垣の演説会が終わった時、相原は、短刀で板垣に襲いかかりました。板垣は負傷しました。

相原は、自由党員・内藤魯一によって、取り押さえられました。

「板垣死すとも」の言葉は、内藤が発したという説もあります。

77 The Fukushima Incident and the Chichibu Incident

福島事件と秩父（ちちぶ）事件

① The governor (県令) of *Fukushima* Prefecture, *Mishima Michitsune*, placed great burden (大きな負担をかけた) on the farmers due to road construction (道路建設). ② The members of the Liberal Party and farmers rose against (〜に対して立ち上がった) *Mishima's* tyranny (圧政). ③ Several thousands of common people (民衆) rushed (押し寄せた) to the police station in November of 1882. ④ The people were dispersed (追い散らされた) by police and the leader was under arrest (逮捕された). ⑤ This is called "the *Fukushima* Incident" (福島事件). ⑥ The *Chichibu* region (秩父地方) in *Saitama* Prefecture developed a silk-raising industry (養蚕業) and was famous for (〜で有名な) raw silk (生糸) and silk fabric (絹織物). ⑦ However, the price of raw silk went down due to serious recession (深刻な不況) under the *Matsukata* Finance Administration (松方財政), and the farmers ran up a debt. ⑧ The farmers started an armed uprising together with the members of the Liberal Party against the government in October of 1884. ⑨ They attacked loan sharks and fought with the police. ⑩ The government dispatched an army and the uprising was suppressed. ⑪ This is called "the *Chichibu* Incident".

借金を重ねた　武装蜂起　襲った　高利貸し　派遣した　暴動　しずまった

和訳

①福島県の県令・三島通庸(みしまみちつね)は、道路工事のため、農民に大きな負担をかけていました。②三島の圧政に対し、自由党員や農民らが立ち上がりました。③1882年11月、数千人の民衆が警察署に押し寄せました。④民衆は警官に追い散らされ、指導者は逮捕されました。⑤これを「福島事件」といいます。⑥埼玉県秩父地方は養蚕業(ようさんぎょう)が発達し、生糸や絹織物の産地でした。⑦しかし、松方財政による深刻な不景気で生糸の価格が下がり、農民は借金を重ねていました。⑧1884年10月、農民たちは自由党員とともに政府に対して武装蜂起(ぶそうほうき)しました。⑨彼らは高利貸(こうりが)しを襲い、警官隊と交戦しました。⑩政府は軍隊を投入し、暴動をしずめました。⑪これを「秩父事件」といいます。

78 The First Prime Minister, Ito Hirobumi

初代内閣総理大臣・伊藤博文（いとうひろぶみ）

① *Ito Hirobumi* was born to（～に生まれた） a poor farming house（貧しい農家） in the *Choshu* Domain. ② He went to *Shokason Juku* and was taught by *Yoshida Shoin*. ③ He was pleased by（目をかけられた） *Kido Takayoshi* and *Takasugi Shinsaku* and joined the movement of expelling foreigners（攘夷運動） and the anti-shogunate movements（倒幕運動）. ④ He joined the *Iwakura* Mission in Western Countries（岩倉米欧使節団） as a sub-missionary（副使） in the *Meiji* government and visited（視察した） western countries. ⑤ After the passing of（～亡きあと） *Saigo Takamori*, *Okubo Toshimichi*, *Kido Takayoshi* and others, he became a key figure（中心人物） in the government. ⑥ He visited Europe to examine（調査する） the Constitution（憲法） in 1882. ⑦ After returning,

he arranged the cabinet system in order and took the
整えた 内閣制度 ～に就任した
position of the first Prime Minister. ⑧ He also worked
初代内閣総理大臣 ～に取り組んだ
on making the draft of the Constitution and established
憲法草案 制定した
The Constitution of the Empire of Japan. ⑨ He was
大日本帝国憲法
killed by a Korean activist, An Jungun in Harbin
活動家 安重根
(China) in 1909.

和訳

①伊藤博文は、長州藩の貧しい農家に生まれました。②松下村塾に通い、吉田松陰の教えを受けました。③木戸孝允や高杉晋作に目をかけられ、攘夷運動や討幕運動に加わりました。④明治政府では岩倉米欧使節団に副使として参加し、欧米を視察しました。⑤西郷隆盛、大久保利通、木戸孝允らが亡きあとは、政府の中心人物となりました。⑥1882年、憲法調査のためヨーロッパに渡りました。⑦帰国後、内閣制度を整え、初代内閣総理大臣に就任しました。⑧憲法草案作成にも取り組み、大日本帝国憲法を制定しました。⑨1909年、ハルビンで韓国人の活動家・安重根に殺害されました。

79

The Issuance of The Constitution of the Empire of Japan

大日本帝国憲法の発布

This is the constitution I made myself.
私がつくった憲法だ。
1889年2月11日、大日本帝国憲法は発布されました。
Hurray! Hurray!
ばんざーい！ばんざーい！
多くの国民が憲法発布を祝いました。
We have become the first constitutional monarchy in Asia.
アジア初の立憲君主国になったよ。
大日本帝国憲法は、アジア初の近代憲法でした。

80 The First Imperial Diet
第1回帝国議会

① The first general election for the members of the
第1回総選挙 衆議院議員

House of Representatives was held on July 1, 1890.
行なわれた

② Men who were 25 years and over and paid more
満25歳以上 15円以上

than 15 yen in direct national taxes, were given the
直接国税

right to vote. ③ The number of voters were 1.1% of
選挙権 有権者

the total population, which was accounting to about
総人口

only 450,000 people. ④ In the first general election,
総選挙

the members of the Opposing Party (People's Party),
野党(民党)

mainly consisting of the members of the Liberal Party
〜を中心とする 自由党

and the Constitutional Reform Party, won more than
立憲改進党 占めた 過半数

half of the seats. ⑤ The first Imperial Diet was held
議席 第1回帝国議会

on November 29, 1890. ⑥ The Imperial Diet adopted
採用した

the bicameral system which consisted of the House of
二院制 ～で成り立った 衆議院

Representatives and the House of Lords. ⑦ The
貴族院

members of the House of Representatives were chosen
～で選ばれた

in the election by the nation. ⑧ The members of the
国民

House of Lords consisted of Imperial families,
皇族

noblemen, high-income tax payers and the members
華族 高額納税者 勅選議員

who were appointed by the Emperor.

和訳

①1890年7月1日、第1回衆議院議員総選挙が行なわれました。②選挙権が与えられたのは、直接国税（こくぜい）を15円以上納める満25歳以上の男性でした。③これは、有権者は総人口の1.1%、約45万人にすぎませんでした。④第1回総選挙では、自由党や立憲改進党を中心とする野党（民党）が議席の過半数を占めました。⑤1890年11月29日、第1回帝国議会が開かれました。⑥帝国議会は、衆議院と貴族院の二院制を採っていました。⑦衆議院議員は、国民による選挙で選ばれました。⑧貴族院議員は、皇族・華族や高額納税者と勅選（ちょくせん）議員から成っていました。

おさらいクイズ

【問題1】次の英語が表わす日本語を、あとのア〜ウから選びなさい。

① the Cabinet System
② the Opposing Party
③ the Constitutional Reform Party

ア 立憲改進党　　イ 野党　　ウ 内閣制度

【問題2】次の日本語が表わす英語を、あとのア〜ウから選びなさい。

① 自由民権運動
② 集会条例
③ 国会

ア the Freedom and People's Rights Movement
イ the National Diet
ウ assembly regulations

【問題3】次の英文が説明している人物は誰でしょう。あとのア〜ウから選びなさい。

He worked on making the draft of the constitution and established the Constitution of the Empire of Japan.

ア 伊藤博文　　イ 大隈重信　　ウ 植木枝盛

【問題4】次の英文を訳しなさい。

The Liberal Party were radicals.

【答え1】①ウ　②イ　③ア　【答え2】①ア　②ウ　③イ　【答え3】ア
【答え4】自由党は急進的でした。

英単語・英熟語集

本書に掲載された中から
300語をPick up!

［(p.197)：本書内の掲載ページ　類：類義語　反：反意語　派：派生語
［名］：派生語の品詞(この場合は名詞)］

英単語

[A]

abandon 動詞 捨てる(p.71)、放棄する

abolish 動詞 廃止する(p.66·98·123)　派 abolishable[形]、abolishment[名]

accompany 動詞 ともなう(p.70·160)、付き添う

acquire 動詞 得る(p.124)、身につける　派 acquisition[名]

administration 名詞 政府(p.52·176)、政治、管理
派 administer[動]

adopt 動詞 養子にする(p.58)、認可する、採用する(p.101·138)
派 adoption[名]

adoption 名詞 採用(p.149)、実行　派 adopt[動]

adore 動詞 慕う(p.112)、敬愛する

advantageous 形容詞 有利な(p.127)　派 advantage[動]

afterward 副詞 その後(p.14·145)、あとで

agriculture 名詞 農業(p.120)、農耕　派 agricultural[形]

alliance 名詞 同盟(p.54·78)、協調

although 接続詞 けれども(p.20·65·112)、にもかかわらず
類 though

ambitious 形容詞 大志のある(p.158)、野望に燃えている
派 ambition[名]

amount 名詞 (the～)総計(p.128)、総額、要旨

anticipate 動詞 予想する(p.63)、～の先手を打つ
派 anticipated[形]、anticipative[形]、anticipatively[副]、anticipator[名]
appear 動詞 姿を現わす(p.12·59·82)　反 disappear
派 appearance[名]
arbitration 名詞 調停(p.122)、仲裁　類 mediation
※mediationより法的強制力を持つ
arrange 動詞 整える(p.179)、手配する　派 arranged[形]、arrangement[名]
arson 名詞 放火(p.68)
authority 名詞 権威(p.30)、権限(p.97)　派 authorize[動]
authorize 動詞 公認する(p.87)、認定する　派 authority[名]
avoid 動詞 避ける(p.15·74)　類 escape

[B]

basically 副詞 もともと(p.132)、基本的に、本来は
派 basic[形]
bastard 名詞 (無礼な)やつ(p.174)
bicameral 形容詞 二院制の(p.183)　反 unicameral
blame 動詞 非難する(p.114)、責める　類 condemn　反 praise
burden 名詞 負担(p.129·176)、重荷

[C]

categorize 動詞 分類する(p.104·152)　派 categorization[名]
certify 動詞 証明する(p.128)、認定する　派 certifier[名]
classify 動詞 分類する(p.104)、区分する　派 classification[名]
collapse 動詞 崩れる(p.69)
colloquialism 名詞 口語体(p.156)　派 colloquial[形]
colonize 動詞 植民地にする(p.14·103)
combine 動詞 組み合わせる(p.152)、提携する　派 combination[名]
commit 動詞 (罪などを)犯す(p.18·65)、かかわる

commonly 副詞 一般に(p.157)　反 uncommonly
compel 動詞 強制する(p.13)、強いる　類 force
派 compulsion[名]、compulsory[形]
compensation 名詞 賠償金(p.122)、補償　派 compensational[形]
completely 副詞 完全に(p.22·69·99)、徹底的に
confrontation 名詞 対決(p.76)、直面　派 confront[動]
conquer 動詞 征服する(p.92·168)、得る　派 conqueror[名]、conquest[名]
conscription 名詞 徴兵(p.105·118)
consider 動詞 考える(p.31)、みなす(p.46·154)
派 consideration[名]
consist 動詞 ～から成り立つ(p.70·172)
constitution 名詞 憲法(p.52·91·166)、構成、制定
派 constitute[動]、constitutional[形]
construction 名詞 建設(p.144·176)、建築物　派 construct[動]
contradict 動詞 相反する(p.165)、矛盾する、反論する
派 contradiction[名]
contribute 動詞 貢献する(p.51·145)、与える、提案する
派 contribution[名]
corruption 名詞 腐敗(p.115)、堕落
creation 名詞 作成(p.105)、創作　派 create[動]
criticism 名詞 非難(p.24)、批判(p.170)、批評
criticize 動詞 批判する(p.165)

[D]

debt 名詞 借金(p.177)
decline 動詞 断わる(p.30)、下落する(p.139)、傾く　名詞 衰え(p.59)
decree 名詞 法令(p.15)、布告(p.90)
dedicate 動詞 ささげる(p.160)
defeat 動詞 負かす(p.14·44·77)、くじく　派 defeatism[名]、defeatist[名]

deficit 名詞 赤字(p.132)、不足
demand 動詞 要求する(p.14·165)　類 claim
※demandは命令、権力にもとづいて要求する。claimは自分の当然の権利として要求する。
devote 動詞 ささげる(p.51·154)、専念する　派 devotion[名]
diet 名詞 国会(p.166·170)
diplomatic 形容詞 外交的な(p.110·161)、外交上の
派 diplomatically[副]
discriminate 動詞 差別する(p.104)、区別する
派 discriminator[名]、discriminately[副]
discuss 動詞 協議する(p.19·67)、話し合う　派 discussion[名]
dispatch 動詞 派遣する(p.44·109·122)、発送する
dispute 名詞 論争(p.111)、議論
dissatisfy 動詞 不満を抱かせる(p.108·169)、不快にさせる
distinguish 動詞 目立つ(p.92)、区別する
派 distinguishable[形]、distinguishably[副]
disturbance 名詞 騒ぎ(p.35)、混乱
※riotの遠回し語
domestic 形容詞 国内の(p.110)、国内産の　反 foreign
派 domesticate[動]、domesticity[名]
draft 名詞 下書き(p.70)、草案(p.172)

[E]

edict 名詞 勅諭(p.94·171)、命令
effect 名詞 影響(p.82)、効果　派 effective[形]
election 名詞 選挙(p.182)、投票
encourage 動詞 働きかける(p.62)、はげます　派 encouragement[名]
enlightenment 名詞 啓発(p.143·154)
envoy 名詞 外交使節(p.110·144)、特使
equipment 名詞 設備(p.166)、備品　派 equip[動]
essential 形容詞 欠かせない(p.144)、きわめて重要な
派 essence[名]

establish 動詞 設立する(p.51·66·90)、設ける
派 establishment[名]
examine 動詞 調査する(p.178)、試験をする　派 examination[名]
exchangeable 形容詞 交換できる(p.131)、取り替えられる
派 exchangeability[名]
exempt 動詞 免除する(p.119)　派 exemption[名]
existence 名詞 生活(p.121)、暮らし、存在、実在
expand 動詞 伸ばす(p.136)、広げる、膨張する　派 expansion[名]
expect 動詞 期待する(p.34·62·136)、予期する
expel 動詞 追放する(p.31·170)、排出する

[F]
favorable 形容詞 有利な(p.16)、好都合の
feudalistic 形容詞 封建主義的な(p.156)　派 feudal[形]、feudality[名]
figure 名詞 人物(p.178)
force 動詞 強いる、強要する(p.14·32·126)　名詞 軍隊(p.50)、
武力(p.62·110)、一隊　類 compel　派 forced[形]、forcible[形]
fortune 名詞 富、財産(p.137)
furthermore 副詞 さらに(p.32·126)、そのうえに　類 besides

[G]
gain 動詞 得る(p.42)、手に入れる　反 lose
gather 動詞 集まる(p.112)、増大する
gradually 副詞 しだいに(p.121)、だんだんと　派 gradual[形]
graduate 動詞 卒業する(p.21·155)　派 graduation[名]
greatness 名詞 すばらしさ(p.154)、偉大さ

[I]
identity 名詞 身分(p.121)、自己同一性、同一であること
派 identical[形]、identify[動]
ignore 動詞 無視する(p.26)　類 neglect

inconvenience 名詞 不都合(p.148)、不便　反 convenience
派 inconvenient[形]
indiscriminately 副詞 無差別に(p.48)　反 discriminately
派 indiscriminate[形]、indiscriminateness[名]
individual 名詞 個人(p.172)
individualism 名詞 個人主義(p.156)　反 totalitarianism
inherit 動詞 受け継ぐ(p.20)、相続する　派 inheritance[名]
initiate 動詞 着手する(p.128)、始める　派 initiative[名·形]
insecure 形容詞 不安定な(p.52)、不確かな　反 secure
派 insecurely[副]
insolent 形容詞 無礼な(p.114)、ごうまんな　類 rude
派 insolently[副]
instead 副詞 その代わりに(p.112)
insurance 名詞 保険(p.135)　派 insure[動]
intend 動詞 意図する(p.30)、もくろむ　派 intent[名 · 形]、intention[名]
intensify 動詞 ～を強める(p.76)、激しくする
invent 動詞 考案する(p.147)、発明する　派 invention[名]、inventor[名]
investigate 動詞 調査する(p.155)、取り調べる
派 investigation[名]
issue 動詞 公布する(p.84·90)、発行する(p.128)　派 issuer[名]

[L]

lead 動詞 率いる(p.12·50)、引き起こす(p.35)、導く　派 leader[名]
lecturer 名詞 講師(p.154)、教官　派 lecture[名]
liberal 形容詞 自由主義の(p.172·174)
liberalism 名詞 自由主義(p.156)　派 liberal[形]
liberation 名詞 解放(p.104)
literature 名詞 文学(p.157)
luxurious 形容詞 豪華な(p.160)、ぜいたく好みの
派 luxuriousness[名]、luxury[名]

[M]

maintain 動詞 維持する(p.36·103)、整備する、養う
派 maintenance[名]
manage 動詞 管理する(p.152)、取り扱う　派 manager[名]、management[名]
meanwhile 副詞 そのあいだ(p.24)　派 meantime[名]
mention 動詞 挙げる(p.72)、～について述べる
moderate 名詞 穏健派(p.172)
modernization 名詞 近代化(p.49·110)　派 modernize[動]、modernizer[名]
monarchy 名詞 君主国(p.181)、君主制
moreover 副詞 そのうえ(p.18)、さらに(p.170)
mutual 形容詞 相互的な(p.55)、共通の

[N]

nationwide 形容詞 全国的な(p.105)　副詞 全国的に(p.146)
negotiation 名詞 交渉(p.110·160)、折衝　派 negotiate[動]
nucleus 名詞 中心(p.66)、核心

[O]

obedience 名詞 服従(p.47·78)、従順　反 disobedience
obey 動詞 従う(p.74)、守る　反 disobey
objection 名詞 異議(p.125)、不服　類 opposition
反 agreement　派 object[動]
occupy 動詞 占拠する(p.48·76)、占領する(p.122·126)、ふさぐ
occur 動詞 起こる(p.14·82·138)　類 happen
派 occurrence[名]
offer 動詞 申し出る(p.52)、勧める
opportunity 名詞 機会(p.31·126·161)、好機
oppose 動詞 対抗する(p.24·122)、反対する(p.110)
派 opposite[形]、opposition[名]

outflow 名詞 流出(p.130)　反 inflow
outstanding 形容詞 優秀な(p.92·153)、傑出している　類 standout
overthrow 動詞 転覆させる(p.52·62·92)、廃止する

[P]
parent 名詞 母体(p.172)、親
parliament 名詞 議会(p.52·91)
peasant 名詞 農民(p.50)、小作農
permission 名詞 許可(p.18)、認可　派 permit[動]
persuasion 名詞 説得(p.35)、確信、信念
petition 名詞 嘆願書(p.168)、申し立て
physically 副詞 肉体的に(p.22)　派 physical[形]
please 動詞 気に入る(p.178)
politician 名詞 政治家(p.164)　派 politic[形]、political[形·名]
population 名詞 人口(p.182)、住民　派 populate[動]
predecessor 名詞 前身(p.146)、前任者
prepare 動詞 用意する(p.27·43)、立案する(p.173)
prevent 動詞 防ぐ(p.35)、中止させる　派 prevention[名]
privilege 名詞 特権(p.107)、恩恵　動詞 特権を与える(p.108)
proceed 動詞 進む(p.62)、続ける
procession 名詞 行列(p.38)、行進　派 proceed[動]
promote 動詞 促進する(p.32·84·160)、奨励する　派 promotion[名]、promoter[名]、promotional[形]、promotive[形]
property 名詞 所有物(p.167·170)、資産　派 proper[形]
propose 動詞 提案する(p.52·62)、申し込む
protest 動詞 抗議する(p.73)、主張する
派 protestation[名]
purchase 動詞 購入する(p.56)、獲得する

[R]

radical 形容詞 急進的な(p.21·33·170)、過激な 反 conservative
派 radically[副]

recession 名詞 不況(p.139·176)、後退

recognize 動詞 認める(p.16·122) 派 recognition[名]

recommend 動詞 推薦する(p.22·58·144)

reconstruction 名詞 復興(p.154)、再建

recruitment 名詞 (新会員の)募集(p.53)、補充

regenerate 動詞 一新する(p.94)、よみがえらせる
派 regenerator[名]

regime 名詞 政権(p.62)

region 名詞 地方(p.78·120·150)、地域 派 regional[形]

regulation 名詞 条例(p.128·131·170)、規則 類 law

reinforce 動詞 強化する(p.100)、補強する

relationship 名詞 関係(p.49)、結びつき 派 relation[名]、
relate[動]、relative[形]

religion 名詞 宗教(p.84)

remarkable 形容詞 めざましい(p.161)、注目すべき
反 unremarkable

remarkably 副詞 著しく(p.30)、非常に 派 remarkable[形]

reply 動詞 返事をする(p.12)
※answerより堅い語

represent 動詞 ～のしるしである(p.68)、象徴する
派 representation[名]、representative[形]

require 動詞 必要とする(p.54·150)、要求する
派 requirement[名]

residence 名詞 駐在(p.16)、居住(p.104) 派 residential[形]

resign 動詞 辞職する(p.67) 類 retire

respectively 副詞 それぞれ(p.137)、めいめいに 類 each
派 respective[形]

rest 名詞 残り(p.73) 動詞 ～にかかっている(p.174)、次第である

revere 動詞 崇敬する(p.32)、あがめる 類 respect

revise 動詞 改正する(p.102)、変える 派 revision[名]
robbery 名詞 強盗(p.68)、盗難 派 rob[動]
roughly 副詞 およそ(p.148)、概略で 派 rough[形]
rumor 名詞 うわさ(p.83)、流言

[S]
scholar 名詞 学者(p.20)
secure 動詞 確保する(p.98)、守る、保証する 反 insecure
派 security[名]
seek 動詞 求める(p.71)、～しようと努める
seriously 副詞 深刻に(p.38)、本気で 派 serious[形]
settle 動詞 移住させる(p.98)、落ち着く(p.146) 派 settlement[名]
severe 形容詞 痛烈な(p.48·139)、厳しい 派 severely[副]
sharply 副詞 ひどく(p.82)、急に 派 sharp[形]
siege 名詞 包囲攻撃(p.74)
similar 形容詞 類似した(p.16)、同様の 類 same
派 similarity[名] similitude[名]
sovereignty 名詞 主権(p.174)
spread 動詞 広まる(p.44·86·146) 名詞 普及(p.150)、広がり
stricken 形容詞 傷ついた(p.136)
strictly 副詞 厳しく(p.24)、厳密に 派 strict[形]
strife 名詞 争い(p.92·168)、闘争
submit 動詞 提出する(p.168)、意見を述べる
派 submission[名]
suburb 名詞 (the ～s)郊外(p.68) 反 urban 派 suburban[形]
sufficient 形容詞 十分な(p.134)、足りる 類 enough
派 sufficiently[副]
suggest 動詞 提案する(p.36)、示す 派 suggestion[名]、
suggestive[形]
supervision 名詞 管理(p.36)、監督 派 supervise[動]、
supervisory[形]
supply 動詞 供給する(p.16) 類 provide

surrender 動詞 降伏する(p.56·79)、明け渡す(p.75)
名詞 明け渡し(p.76·92)
survey 動詞 測量する(p.126)、調査する、概観する
suspect 動詞 疑う(p.159)、怪しいと思う
swear 動詞 誓う(p.70)
sweep 動詞 圧勝する(p.57)、一掃する、席巻する

[T]
terrible 形容詞 ひどい(p.42)、恐ろしい 派 terribly[副]、terribleness[名]
therefore 副詞 そのために(p.104·129·148)、その結果
throne 名詞 皇位(p.90)、王座、王位
throughout 前置詞 ～のいたるところに(p.71)
tribute 名詞 献上品(p.122·144)、貢物
trigger 動詞 誘発する(p.170)、引き金となる
tyranny 名詞 圧政(p.176)、暴政

[U]
unfamiliar 形容詞 慣れない(p.106)、親しくない
派 unfamiliarity[名]、unfamiliarly[副]
unify 動詞 統一する(p.130)、～をひとつにする 類 integrate
派 unification[名]
uproar 名詞 騒動(p.171)
urge 動詞 強要する(p.13)、主張する(p.166)
utilize 動詞 利用する(p.30) 派 utilizer[名]
utterly 副詞 すっかり(p.45)、完全に
※良い意味ではgreatly、entirely。通常、否定的または悪い意味合いの語とともに用いられる。

[V]
victim 名詞 被害者(p.65)、犠牲者
vote 動詞 投票する(p.182)

[W]

wealth 名詞 富(p.103)、財産　派 wealthy[形]

wealthy 形容詞 裕福な(p.134·172)　類 rich　反 poor
派 wealth[名]

withdraw 動詞 撤退させる(p.47·122)、引く、取り消す

within 副詞 ～の中で(p.32·110·170)　反 without

witness 動詞 目撃する(p.39)、証言をする

worship 動詞 崇拝する(p.84)

英熟語

a number of　多数の(p.132)、若干数の

after a while　やがて(p.165)

agree to　同意する(p.13·16)、賛成する　類 consent

apart from　～は別として(p.152)、～はさておき　類 aside from

as a result　その結果として(p.17·67·126)

as well as　～と同様に(p.98)、～をしながら(p.120)、～だけでなく

at once　すぐに(p.56)、ただちに

at the end of　～の終わり(p.78·130)

at the mouth　入口(p.12)

be applied　適用される(p.16)、応用される

be involved in　～に携わる(p.134)、参加する

belong to　～に属する(p.122)

break out　発生する(p.44)、勃発する

burn down　焼き払う(p.108)、全焼する

carry out　決行する(p.40·92·168)、運び出す　類 execute、perform

catch up with　～に追いつく(p.103·150)

come to an end　おさまる(p.139)、終わる

come to light　明るみに出る(p.166)

compete with ～と肩を並べる(p.96)、張り合う

count on ～を頼りにする(p.56)、～を当てにする

crack down on ～を取り締まる(p.24·170)、弾圧する

crop failure 凶作(p.82)

cut down 削減する(p.138)

day to day 日々の(p.139)

due to ～のために(p.63·98·149)

engage in ～に携わる(p.97)、従事する

enough to 十分な(p.96)

fight back 反撃する(p.57·126)、抵抗する

fire up 盛り上がる(p.169)、かきたてる

for several years 数年間(p.82)

for the first time はじめて(p.144)

get in the way ～の邪魔になる(p.38)

get injure 負傷する(p.33)

go abroad 海外へ行く(p.20·72) 反 at home

head for ～へ向かう(p.34)

in addition to ～に加えて(p.93·160)、～であるうえに

in contrast これに対し(p.148)、対照的に

in order to ～するために(p.34·76·94)

in the beginning of ～の初期(p.132)

in those days 当時(p.132·146)

instead of ～の代わりに(p.123)、～ではなくて

later on のちに(p.147) 反 earlier on

make use of ～を利用する(p.24·36)

on the other hand これに対して(p.124)、他方では

own judgment 独断(p.18)

participate in ～に参加する(p.134)、加わる

react against 反発する(p.33)

regardless of ～に関係なく(p.50·70·156)、～にかかわらず

rouse oneself 決起する(p.108)、発奮する

run away 逃げる(p.41·72)
run up (借金などが)重なる(p.177)、かさむ
take place 起こる(p.122·170)、行なわれる
take time 時間をかける(p.166)
the following year 翌年(p.12·83·105) 類 the next year
throw away ～を捨てる(p.85·154)、無駄に費やす 類 discard
track down 追いつめる(p.46)
under arrest 逮捕されて(p.176)
with all one's might 全力で(p.36)
with reference to ～にならって(p.100·166)、～に関して
yield to ～に屈する(p.32)、従う

祥伝社黄金文庫

すらすら読める！英語対訳・幕末維新史

平成24年7月30日　初版第1刷発行

監修者　木村幸比古
英文監訳者　Marilyn Lo
発行者　竹内和芳
発行所　祥伝社
〒101－8701
東京都千代田区神田神保町3－3
電話　03（3265）2084（編集部）
電話　03（3265）2081（販売部）
電話　03（3265）3622（業務部）
http://www.shodensha.co.jp/
印刷所　堀内印刷
製本所　積信堂

　ISBN978-4-396-31585-6 C0182

祥伝社黄金文庫

小池直己
新TOEIC®TEST 650点を約束する20のツボ
1問20秒 即答トレーニング。スピード力をつけ、20のツボで弱点をあぶり出せば、一気に実力UP！

中村澄子
新TOEIC®テスト スコアアップ135のヒント
最強のTOEICテスト攻略法。基本から直前・当日対策まで、もっとも効率的な勉強法はコレだ！

石田 健
1日1分！英字新聞チャレンジ
2012年版最新時事ニュースで英語を学べ！ TOEIC、就活対策にも最適。

荒井弥栄
ビジネスで信頼されるファーストクラスの英会話
元JAL国際線CAの人気講師が、ネイティブにも通用するワンランク上の「英語」をレッスン！

晴山陽一
即効！ビジネス英単語たった300
1日10題！ クイズを問くだけで、わずか1カ月でビジネスに必要な英単語が身につく最効率の問題集！

シグリッド・H・塩谷
アメリカの子供はどう英語を覚えるか
アメリカ人の子供も英語をまちがえながら覚えていく。子供に戻った気分で、気楽にどうぞ。